ON EARTH
AS IT IS IN
ADVERTISING?

Moving from Commercial Hype
to Gospel Hope

Sam Van Eman

Brazos Press
Grand Rapids, Michigan

© 2005 by Sam Van Eman

Published by Brazos Press
a division of Baker Publishing Group
P.O. Box 6287, Grand Rapids, MI 49516-6287
www.brazospress.com

Printed in the United States of America

Library of Congress Cataloging-in-Publication Data
Van Eman, Sam, 1973–
   On earth as it is in advertising : moving from commercial hype to gospel hope /
Sam Van Eman.
       p.   cm.
   Includes bibliographical references.
   ISBN 1-58743-136-X (pbk.)
   1. Advertising. 2. Advertising—Churches. 3. Christianity—Influence. I. Title.
HF5823.V26 2005
659.19′25—dc22   2005003179

SimGospel (sim-gäs-pəl)
  n. all messages that simulate the biblical narrative through advertising and popular media for the purpose of selling products and ideas.

Contents

Acknowledgments

Julie, I had a whirl of a time writing, but it was often at your expense. I am honored to be your husband, and I recognize, with great pleasure, that your long string of green lights made this project possible. Emma and Alice and I are madly in love with you.

Byron Borger, I like it when people say, "Oh, *Byron* helped you on this? Wow . . . what was that like? What did he say?" I think every writer (and reader) should sit under your tutelage, if only to be inspired to see books as windows to the kingdom. What a privilege to receive the attention of a connoisseur and the genius behind Hearts and Minds Books.

Lisa Foose, I don't know anyone who says it like you say it. You are a truth-teller extraordinaire. When you read the manuscript, you saw behind my words and raised questions about the writer who produced them. This kind of spiritual insight is what Julie and I cherish most about you. Please, keep reading!

Chris Cooke, besides being a friend, you are an effective campus minister with an affinity to good books. For these reasons, I consider it a treat to have had your student-centered eyes scan my pages. (To you, Dave and Scott, three cheers for Limey-ville!)

Jean Kilbourne, you are a gifted woman and a genuine champion of truth in the ad world. Thank you for sharing your convictions with thousands of college students, and also for giving me a chance.

Rodney Clapp, you chiseled at my writing with grace and expertise. Byron informed me that you were a superb editor, and working with you has only confirmed this.

Dave Westerlund, you told me that if I read Jean Kilbourne's *Can't Buy My Love,* I would never see advertising the same. Your statement could not have been more true. I have enjoyed "ruining" the media perspectives of many friends and students with the same advice ever since.

Steve Washek, in a tiny office with no windows (and sometimes against your wishes), you let me run free, unbounded with my gifts. You took this Protestant under your Catholic wing and strengthened my commitment toward healing in the church. While I still don't know how to do "check req's," I've been closer to the pope than you, and this must count for something!

Christine Lundt, you are a brilliant woman with a marvelous sense of humor. Thank you for being a sage as well as my human thesaurus.

Ryan McElhiney, you read this before it had an introduction or a conclusion. It must have felt like catching the middle ten minutes of a movie and then being asked for a review. You are a patient friend.

Mom, I doubt Mrs. Emery ever knew I read Hardy Boy mysteries inside of my fourth-grade desk, but you did, and I don't think you cared—you were just thrilled that I was reading. It's possible that growing up with you howling through Erma Bombeck stories made me wonder what power black print on white pages really held. But most important, as I think about *The Chronicles of Narnia,* I realize that you taught me how to stand willingly under the claws of Aslan.

Grace to all of you who serve as partners in our ministry. Your support moves us forward, and we are deeply grateful.

Introduction

Mike Hasko was twenty years old and still didn't have his driver's license. This seemed a bit odd for a college student, but as a sophomore living on campus, I guess he had little need for transportation. Mike was also in a small group I facilitated on the intersection of faith and culture. When he finally decided to take his driver's test, I didn't expect it would have an impact on our group, but it did. It all started with the results of his eye exam:

"I'm sorry, Mr. Hasko. You will need to see the doctor before you can drive. You failed the eye test."

"My eyes are fine," Mike said. "Maybe there's something wrong with your machine."

"Mr. Hasko, I assure you there is nothing wrong with our machines."

"Well, I'm certain that my eyes are perfect. I'd like to take it again to prove it."

The instructor agreed, and Mike proceeded to fail just as miserably.

Disgruntled and still in disbelief, Mike made an appointment with an optometrist. He went and, of course, was told the same thing. So the doctor gave him a pair of glasses.

To Mike's amazement, the glasses made a radical difference. He was mostly surprised at how odd things looked. At first, he didn't even say that he could see better—only different. He left the office that day marveling at how neckties and road signs and restaurant menus looked so much sharper. He was perceiving everything in a new way.

Perhaps this is the case for anyone who gets new glasses (I don't wear them), but when Mike shared this story with our group, it caused us to reflect on the very nature of learning:

The funny thing was that I swore the eye machine at the driver's center was a fluke. I didn't even believe the optometrist at first. I was so convinced I could see well that glasses didn't make any sense. But when I actually put them on, the truth became so apparent that it shocked me. I've taken eye exams before. I guess my sight went bad slowly enough since then that I didn't notice.

After getting over my own surprise at this account, I asked, "Mike, how could eyesight and your glasses story lend itself to the Christian content of this small group?" It took him only a brief moment to make the connection, and he said:

It has everything to do with why we need this kind of study. Because we consume more movies than scripture and listen to more TV actors than Jesus, and because we rarely put an ounce of thought into our interactions with popular culture, the messages get mixed up. We lose focus on God, which means that everything we see is from a blurred point of view. When all we hear in advertising is "Me, Me, Me," who we really are gets blown out of proportion. We forget that Jesus calls us to love others, and we end up replacing him with something less.

For Mike, this was an immediate intellectual conversion. Most of us, however, need more time.

For twenty-five years, my time in front of the TV was mindless. Sitcoms and cartoons were of special interest to me, and I watched them a lot. As a child, I awoke early on Saturday mornings to watch Looney Tunes and the Coyote's endless pursuit of the Road Runner. I remember sitting on the couch with my sisters to watch *The Cosby Show, Growing Pains,* and countless episodes of *The Dukes of Hazzard.* Between shows, we laughed at commercials and sang fast-food jingles; we memorized ad lines and used them in conversations: "Wake up all you sleepyheads, Colgate gets you out of bed" and "Where's the beef?" Without much care, we allowed TV to serve as a very influential (and unchallenged) source of entertainment. My friends did the same, and the content of television became common ground for most of us.

Christianity in our home provided general moral guidance for *what* we consumed, but overall it did not serve in its full capacity regarding *why* and *how* we consumed it. This is perhaps typical in many homes and churches. Teaching children how to think critically about why and how they absorb media is a daunting task, and I am quickly learning this as a parent. I believe that mantras for censorship, like "be careful, little eyes, what you see" and "be careful, little ears, what you hear" are inadequate guides. If our parameters for censorship are simply no foul language, sex, or gratuitous violence, then we are relying on cheap wisdom. This approach to watching TV and commercials is too incomplete to be called meaningful.

In many ways, over two decades of media passed in front of my sisters and friends and me without full Christian engagement. My Sunday school teachers were guilty. My parents were guilty. I was guilty. But so what? Did it have that great of an impact to warrant serious attention and Christian discernment?

I can't say that mindless consumption was unsatisfying, or all of it bad. But as I grew older, a hunger for deeper engagement arose. I never said, "I need to think more *Christianly* about what and how I consume." Rather, I only felt that something was missing in the process. I had a haunting sense that while I consumed entertainment mindlessly, the entertainment itself was not mindless. That is to say, I became convinced that little, if any of it, was produced without meaning, ulterior motives, or the influence of differing worldviews.

Throughout scripture, God affirms specific truths about us and calls us to a way of life that reflects the kingdom Christ prayed for. I could not reconcile this fact with the possibility that advertising—so pervasive in all these media forms—was making its own powerful statements about meaning and the way we ought to live. As a Christian, was I immune to this influence? Most likely, no. Especially since I was haphazard about my consumption. Furthermore, if Jesus claimed to be Lord of all, what implications did his lordship have for the advertising world? What exactly did he mean by requesting God's "will be done on earth as it is in heaven"? (Matt. 6:10).

I didn't really know, but allowing this cultural messaging system to whip by without any substantial interaction or effort to transform it seemed counterproductive to Jesus's words. I was guilty of this, and I still am in too many ways. Mindless consumption is characteristic not only of TV watching, but also of shopping, entertainment, eating, driving, and work. I was beginning to see this in me, and I wanted to be rid of it. I wanted God to be bigger than Sundays and church. And I wanted the influence of Jesus to be far stronger than the hundreds of thousands of ads I was seeing and hearing.

New glasses

Then they . . . brought him to a meeting of the Areopagus, where they said to him, "May we know what this new teach-

ing is that you are presenting? You are bringing some strange
ideas to our ears, and we want to know what they mean.
(Acts 17:19–20)

In my mid-twenties I began working for a Christian organization that specializes in ministering to college students.
Its employees seemed to have an uncanny ability to be in the
world but not of it as they worked on campus (Jesus prayed
this for the disciples in John 17), and this drew my attention.
They hosted movie discussions with students on a regular
basis. They read *Rolling Stone* and *Christianity Today;* they
listened to Bob Dylan, Dave Matthews, and praise music.
They critiqued all music and literature and film with equal
care, knowing that a Christian label does not guarantee accurate theology, nor does a secular label necessarily mean
valueless content. Simply addressing the "what" in either
secular or Christian media was seen as insufficient for proper
guidance. Why and how, they believed, were also essential
for wisdom to be applied faithfully.

Overall, they seemed well informed on popular culture and
at the same time communicated the Gospel effectively with
students. I wondered how this mix was possible.

Pastor David Cassidy believes that the apostle Paul excelled
in this mix. He calls it the "Areopagus Model" and uses the
Acts passage above as the example. Cassidy states that "Paul
provided an excellent model for engaging the culture and
ideas of his day, showing them the futility of their worldview and using their own notions and words against them.
He was a polemicist extraordinaire."[1] Paul not only had a
passion for telling others about Christ and the kingdom of
God, but understood the times and could apply his faith
with pertinence.

The longer I work with students in particular, the more I
learn how to do this. But I have not done it alone. In addition to mentors and a spiritual director, assistance from valuable resources has caused me to wrestle with this interaction

between culture and faith. Mars Hill Audio was one such resource introduced to me by a friend. Mars Hill "exists to assist Christians who desire to move from thoughtless consumption of modern culture to a vantage point of thoughtful engagement." It is a modern-day example of what Paul did so well. Mars Hill believes that:

> fulfilling the commands to love God and neighbor requires that we pay careful attention to the neighborhood: that is, every sphere of human life. . . . Therefore, living as disciples of Christ pertains not just to prayer, evangelism, and Bible study, but also our enjoyment of literature and music, our use of tools and machines, our eating and drinking, our views on government and economics, and so on."[2]

This and many other resources have forced me to contend with God's sovereignty over all the earth, and they have addressed my hunger for deeper engagement. Every day, I see a little more clearly.

My intent

I want to clarify that within popular culture, no element has more influence than advertising. Even though movies and magazines and other media are prevalent in our society (remember the hours I spent absorbing television?), I want to propose that they have little power on their own. This is because they serve as carriers for advertising's messages.

It may help to imagine advertising as a message distribution center—a pulpit from which varying grades of sermons are preached. Advertising is not MTV, nor is it fitness magazines, football games, grocery stores, or fashion. But it uses these to carry what it has to say. In other words, it is the element that thrives by using popular culture and all forms of media to distribute its messages.

Most often, and most noticeably, advertising poses as itself in venues such as TV commercials and magazine spots for cheese crackers. This is the obvious stuff we think of when someone says "advertising," and it is where we will spend the majority of our time in the following chapters. But advertising also acts covertly when specific, tangible products are not visible or not highlighted. For example, a wardrobe director for a movie may dress the lead actress in a certain brand because the clothing company pays to have this done. Even though nothing is mentioned about it in the film, the style and use of color are still marketed to millions of impressionable viewers.

As we explore these and other levels of how advertising works, you will see that products, values, and ideas are advertised everywhere, usually without our acknowledgment. When we expose ourselves mindlessly to popular culture, we interpret little of it wisely and we permit most of what is advertised to leave residue on our consciousness.

Over the past fifty years or so, advertising has had tremendous effects on American culture. Referring to TV in particular, Neil Postman said, "Twenty years ago, the question, Does television shape culture or merely reflect it? held considerable interest for many scholars and social critics. The question has largely disappeared as television has gradually *become* our culture."[3] What effect does this have on us?

Humans are hungry people, and we long for what only God can provide. However, we are like sheep without a shepherd, willing, as my good friend says, "to keep nibbling along right out of the pasture." Advertisers know this and they cater to it well. The bulk of messaging we receive is laced with half answers for the sake of pushing material goods and increasing company profit. And we consume it without realizing its profound effects on our lives.

On one hand, the biblical narrative offers real solutions to real problems. It defines who we are and what we need, and even presents a way of life that would benefit all people. But on the other, sin hijacks this truly redemptive message and reproduces it in countless TV programs, Saturday morning cartoons, magazine pages, and clothing ads, always leaving us short of real fulfillment.

We talk about issues of the day in our Christian circles, but the louder, more influential, more accepted media voice continues to preach without intelligent rebuttal from the Christian worldview. This hijacked simulation of the Gospel—this *SimGospel*—must be uncovered and countered.

There is a commercial with a young couple sitting together on a couch, telling the camera why Big Lots department store is important to them. They boast of deals found on chairs and love seats, and snuggle close as if a significant change has occurred in their lives. The girl looks at her boyfriend/husband and then at the camera again. Through joyful tears, she says, "The world is so full of emptiness. That's why Big Lots has furniture."

None of us believes that ultimate fulfillment is found at Big Lots. That would be ludicrous. However, when the humor and absurdity of ads disarm our ability to think critically; when peers and coworkers act as conductors of the SimGospel's message; when the lifestyles of the rich and famous are heralded on every magazine cover, every prime-time show, and every advertisement; and when the message is always, "You don't have enough, you are not enough, you need more and better and bigger, you can purchase worth and destiny," then we begin to act as if (even if we don't believe) fulfillment really is possible in a furniture store.

Doesn't this seem strange to you? Yet, I hear the results of it every August when college freshmen arrive:

Me: "Hi. What are you going to study?"
Student: "Pre-pharmacy."
Me: "Oh, yeah? What draws you to that field?"
Student: "I don't know . . . it pays well."
Me: "And?"
Student: "And what?"

Not all say this, but I hear it frequently. A few joyfully surprise me by adding: ". . . and because I believe the pharmaceutical world needs some ethical attention. Mostly, though, I desire to help people."

I minister to college students and thoroughly enjoy it. You will see examples throughout the following pages related to college life, because it is what I know best. Students are inquisitive and unsure, and they spend most of their time trying to define themselves and their futures. They are also media-soaked. In fact, their lifestyles, appearance, and dreams serve as visible parallels to what is happening in the media world. Students are often replications of what is happening on TV, and I see that Postman's words are true.

In four years or so, students graduate and enter a career path, carrying into the world with them either the Gospel message or the counterfeit SimGospel message. And they will leave their marks, respectively. This is a critical time, and I believe that watching movies, reading magazines and books, and engaging students on pop-culture values are significant ways to encourage thinking. I take great joy in knowing that one or two navigational nuggets could be pulled from these pages and used for God's glory.

However, a hot market for advertising thrives wherever there are consumers—not just in college. We all shop. And we all want contentment. Stuart Ewen, author of *All Consuming Images* and professor of media studies, says that "it is in 'leisure' that many people look for satisfaction. One of the most available routes to satisfaction is consumption."[4] When we address our needs through what is advertised—be it a physical product or a lifestyle ideal—we become susceptible to charlatan solutions. This is especially true when buyers enter the marketplace unaware.

God desires for us to find fullness in him, to see him as our reference point for wholeness. I strongly believe that the following material is appropriate for anyone who shops, watches TV, flips through magazines, listens to the radio, or has any regular participation in our media-filled, consumer culture (I think this includes all of us). It is a tool to be used for gaining discernment and for becoming effective, thinking Christians.

In these chapters, I will emphasize the importance of entering the media world with a discerning mind. It is difficult to become healthy and prophetic, as I am sure you know, but God's wisdom will enable us. In chapter 1, I will define the SimGospel by comparing it to the Gospel and then provide concrete examples of its presence in our culture.

I wish to thank you in advance for entering this discussion.

Stolen Goods

The SimGospel defined

Gospel. The word means good news.

It is "something accepted as infallible or as a guiding principle."[1] Typically referring to New Testament writings or to the teachings of Jesus, the Gospel also includes the good news throughout scripture about who we are, who God is, and what purpose we have in his creation.

The good news of both the Old and New Testaments profoundly shapes us. It informs us of God's presence throughout history and reminds us of promises to come. It reveals his magnificent character and the fact—confirmed by his centuries-long patience with sinful people—that he is loving, just, and faithful. With redemption and restoration at its heart, the Gospel provides hope and guidance. Yet, in spite of all this, we have compromised it for our own ends and appear rather committed to a simulated, counterfeit version. How did a substitution come to be and why do we continue to rely on it with such diligence and misdirected faith?

In a world where practically anything can be manufactured and where faith in God is often hard to find and hold on to, simulations seem easy. We may believe the world could be a better place, yet ingredients like security, acceptance, dignity, etc., don't materialize with the flip of a switch. God promises these valuable items, but sometimes it feels like he works too slowly. We want goodness now, and we're willing to settle for second-rate options if the good stuff is too hard to get. Combine our human longings and lack of patience with the motivation for companies to sell products, and what we get is the SimGospel.

The SimGospel is a simulated version of the biblical narrative. It is goodness, borrowed. Like the game SimCity, a computer program that allows the player to create and govern a simulated city, the SimGospel is an imitated means to self-establishment. We follow directly on the autonomous heels of our Eden ancestors by overruling God's intended order and creating our own way of life. We become little gods—creating, establishing, changing, and acting as the sovereign ruler. As with SimCity, we assume transcendence, looking down with power on our own fabrication.

In the Garden of Eden, however, God made the world as *he* wanted it, and he established guidelines intended to bring pleasure to him, unity to us, and harmony to the created order. Following these guidelines would yield a world where place and purpose, service and justice, authenticity and dignity would rule the day. Perhaps there would be no credit cards, make-up, or protective fences to compensate for poor treatment of each other. Unfortunately, this height of behavior is unattainable as sinful people, even though we continually strive for the good it would manifest.

Let me be clear: in the garden we knew and experienced perfect harmony in our relationships with God, each other, and creation. We then assumed autonomy, rejected God's care for us, and sought a more immediate, cheaper form of fulfillment. The memory of our utopian state, however, lingers enough that every day since, we have, like King Solomon, chased after the wind with the hope of restoring the fullness of our human longings. The ensuing chapters will reveal the irony of how diligently the SimGospel, via the advertising world, works to reproduce samples of Eden for our tasting.

To set up our approach to this dialogue, I thought it would be helpful to offer three examples of biblical institutions that give life and breadth to the Gospel, along with their simulated counterparts—their SimGospel counterparts—as portrayed in today's media. The three are relationships, work, and rest. It is important that I mention these in their normative states first, as they will provide a basis for defining the SimGospel. Remember, we are dealing with a borrowed message that simulates life as it should be.

Cornelius Plantinga, in his book *Not the Way It's Supposed to Be: A Breviary of Sin,* proposes that

> sin is a parasite, an uninvited guest that keeps tapping its host for sustenance. Nothing about sin is its own; all its power, persistence, and plausibility are stolen goods. Sin is not really an entity but a spoiler of entities, not an organism but a leech on organisms. Sin does not build shalom; it vandalizes it. In metaphysical perspective, evil offers no true alternative to good, as if the two were equal and opposite qualities. . . . Good is original, independent, and constructive; evil is derivative, dependent, and destructive. To be successful, evil needs what it hijacks from goodness.[2]

First, a look at *relationships.*
"For this reason a man will leave his father and mother and be united to his wife, and they will become one flesh" (Gen. 2:24). Marriage was instituted prior to Adam and Eve's first sin. Husband and wife were intended to complement each other, to *forgo* a life of self-centeredness and to enter

a unified bond of service. The fact that Adam and Eve felt no shame speaks loudly of the relationship they had: no fear regarding appearance, no abuse to cause hiding from each other, and no guilt associated with violating trust. To feel no shame signified an honorable and mutual respect. In other words, each affirmed the worth of the other by giving his or her own.

This is the basis for healthy community, and whether we are married or not, these factors (to their appropriate degrees) are necessary in our relationships with others. Unfortunately, a flip through any popular men's or women's magazine, or an evening of prime-time TV, will quickly reveal that something has gone wrong with the original state. Women are naked, but not honorably. What honor does objectification provide? Men are attracted to women, but not out of dignity. What power or manliness is in that?

However, the desire for the same depth of intimacy Adam and Eve had is what is maligned to sell products today. Countless perfume and cologne ads depict erotic scenes and a sense of intimate connection. Sadly, the fragrance, and not the person, does the attracting. And because the half-naked models are on public display, intimacy is not really present. True intimacy is never possible in a crowd, particularly when that crowd is made of TV viewers and disconnected readers who have no relational investment in the models on display.

In *Can't Buy My Love: How Advertising Changes the Way We Think and Feel,* author Jean Kilbourne critiques a Jovan musk ad. Two standard-looking models are passionately embracing behind the question, "What attracts? This is what attracts." Kilbourne says, "The answer to the question . . . is the perfume being advertised, which means these particular partners are irrelevant. They could easily be with anyone else who happened to be wearing Jovan musk."[3] Nothing about the individuals does the attracting. Intellect, care, sincerity, humor, and honesty are not part of this equation. Intimacy is only simulated.

In many cases, these models have no relationship with each other. They are hired for a quick gig and sent off to kiss someone else for another ad. Intimacy is used as a catch line because we were created for it. We know, somehow, that when paired with honor and dignity and not with shame, intimacy is a key to fulfillment.

Work is a second pre-sin reality set into place by God. Not only did God give responsibility to the couple to care for the garden, but also his own labor was on display for them to admire and emulate. As early as Genesis 4 we learn that Adam and Eve's children had become forerunners to farmers, musicians, and tool manufacturers (Gen. 4:20–22).

Work is, of course, a necessity. But more than that, it is worship as we respond with our talents to do what benefits others for the sake of pleasing God. The problem arises when the objective of work becomes accumulation and personal security at the expense of others less fortunate than us. When this happens, we miss the heart of it, and the SimGospel takes the credit.

I can remember TV commercials where two adjacent suburban yards are divided by a white picket fence. There is a man in each yard, cutting the grass with a certain type of mower. We learn that man A has an average piece of equipment, and man B has an upgrade that not only cuts, but also mulches and self-propels. Man A becomes envious. The picket fence now symbolizes a dividing line of competition. It is clear that man A will need to buy either the same mower as his neighbor or a better one.

More hours at work and more pushing of pencils, all to honor God by making the world a better place? No. In fact, it does not matter what kind of job it is, or how the money is made, so long as the neighbors keep up or stay ahead of each other.

Commercials like this rarely make direct statements about the purpose or value of work. They only misdirect work. They imply a certain meaning—a meaning that strays from God's original intention. The beauty of work as an act of worship and service is simulated as a means of keeping up with the Joneses.

Third, *rest* is a critical part of the Creation story. "By the seventh day God had finished the work he had been doing; so on the seventh day he rested from all his work. And God blessed the seventh day and made it holy, because on it he rested from all the work of creating that he had done" (Gen. 2:2–3).

Rest is a recharging time, a time for solitude, play, and worship. We need rest from labor and occasionally from people, material things, and even ourselves when overconsumption begins to appear in these areas. Anything can be consumed in unhealthy measures. Rest simply provides time to refocus on moderation. Crops need to be rotated to rest the ground; nature in general needs rest from pollution and contamination; children need rest from structured activities; parents need date nights; employees need vacations; cars need oil changes; and malls need to close their doors to our buying frenzies from time to time.

Rest is good, and God-ordained, but as with relationships and work, the SimGospel answers how we should rest with a simulation of what is truly restorative. It says that resting from stress can be handled through smoking cigarettes; debriefing from work is best done at a bar with alcohol; cooling from peer pressure is achieved by shopping; and so on. Moreover, we desire to simplify life, and technology seems to promise that simplification. Ironically, while remote controls were designed to make life easier, I have to sort out four remotes for my TV and stereo.

We microwave breakfast, lunch, and dinner, but only to fill what used to be cooking time with a number of other activities. Where once we may have spent two hours preparing, mixing, adding, slicing, and browning, now we open a package and push a few buttons on the keypad. In the meantime, we clean out the car, take out the trash from all the waste we produce, catch a half-hour TV show, and check e-mail, all in the same two hours.

We drink alcohol and use credit cards because they are presented as commodities for rest. Alcohol enables us to cope with the rigorous demands of consumption. It permits us to drink ourselves into some level of oblivion and find a temporary escape without losing (much) productivity at work. And credit cards frequently become tickets to poverty relief, allegedly placing us in higher socioeconomic groups. But we allow them to haul us into debt and force us into a type of slave labor, where work is no longer a gift but a dictator.

We work harder to keep up with others, and we take fewer vacations. Rest comes in the form of releases that do not slow our lives down but only cause us to believe we are being restored. In the advertising world, we are not told to curb our consumption. That would dent the product industry's profit. Instead, we are encouraged to shop, and therefore to work more (or at least earn more).

In the end, I am saying a very simple thing about these Eden guidelines: the SimGospel takes what was intended for good and reproduces it in a lesser light. Whether intimate relationships, meaningful work, invigorating rest, or anything else God intended, the SimGospel preaches them in a simulated form.

I say "preaches" as if the advertising pulpit has a mind of its own. Ironically, it doesn't. The SimGospel is our own invention. It is an invention very much like the Gospel, just as the game SimCity is very much *like* a city. In this Gospel simulation, we assume control over a set of truths that do not belong to us, and then we program SimGospel "theology" into our culture so that it propagates itself.

The problem? A simulation isn't real. And if it isn't real, then it can't solve real problems, or provide real answers, or produce real fulfillment. It is just a host of empty vows.

Injected meaning

Advertising sells more than material goods. It is laden with alternative messages, and because advertising is everywhere, we are constantly exposed to these messages. Does this exposure affect us? If I see one ad that equates alcohol with finding a date, will I think alcohol is the way to get a date? Of course not. In the same way, a flamingo will not turn pink by eating just one brine shrimp. It is the cumulative effect of thousands upon thousands of ads saying the same basic thing in hundreds of formats via dozens of media forms from toddlerhood until today that has a profound effect. Most of us deny that ads have any personal influence (especially negative), but is that really possible? How much of the stuff filling our cupboards and thoughts is there in large part because of advertising?

My wife and I went without a television for five years. It was the equivalent of cutting off the media's primary blood supply, yet advertising did not disappear. Billboards, magazines, radio ads, the mall, cereal boxes, and friends who wore new styles of blue jeans continued to speak volumes to how we perceived culture. Advertising was everywhere, and it almost always contained messages that set parameters for what the SimGospel calls normal.

When advertising goes beyond informing consumers objectively about products and services, and it cooperates with the SimGospel, then I am concerned. When it offers products—products unable to be sold on their own merit—through the promise of meeting basic human needs, then I am concerned. Stuart Ewen believes that many of the products we see advertised are so void of purpose that "[w]e must inject values because the utility of the product is not enough on its own to buy it."[4] The following magazine ad for Bridgestone tires exemplifies this value injection, even though we may genuinely need tires.

The phrase "A Vision in Black" stands at the center, commanding attention. A shiny wheel and tire dominate the lower left corner of the ad against a black background. And resting on the top curve of the tire and extending out of the picture is a woman's lower leg and foot. *It,* and I cannot say *she,* as this is a dismembered part of her, is tan and very seductive. It is wearing a black stiletto heel whose laces intimately climb the calf to a small clasp. The first two small-print phrases in the bottom right corner read, "Smooth moves" and "Cool curves." After a few more lines, the last one reads, "Isn't technology a kick?"

What the eye sees is the sexy leg, the tire, and the phrase, "A Vision in Black." In reality, the woman—a fantasized vision, since only a leg is visible—has no connection with "technology." While "technology" is meant to refer to the tire, a phrase such as "smooth curves" is obviously not about the product. Mentally, we have been reading descriptions of the woman, so the word *technology*—now attached to her lingering image— confers a nonhuman quality. Computers and advancements in the composition of rubber and tread design are certainly technology, but a woman? Absolutely not.

Furthermore, dismemberment neglects her worth. In this way, she has no emotional depth, no hurts, no dreams, no family, and no intelligence. The remainder of her is not needed. Only the sleek curves and the black leather strap, which arouse a sexual response, are necessary to enhance the tire's utility value. We need tires. Bridgestone sells them. We want intimacy. Bridgestone provides arousal through seduction and the sense that good tires not only give us control over the road, but make us more attractive and appealing as well. Magically, these elements combine, and we are offered much more than a car product.

It is important to make a disclaimer here: not all ads misuse or abuse reality to sell products. It is quite possible that Adam and Eve's growing family would have used advertising eventually, even if they had never been removed from paradise. Providing goods and services requires advertising if only to inform the customer. If I need bread and see a store called *Tom's,* I may not know to enter. However, *Tom's Bakery* tells me what I need to know.

Some products, on the other hand, really have inherently deeper values than their utility worth. A closer look at an orange juice commercial, for example, reveals that orange juice is promoted by attaching health to it. But there is obviously no reason to think that we are being duped. It's true. Orange juice is good for us. Again, if Volvo cars make us think of "safety" because historically they have proven to be safe vehicles, then it is not deceptive for them to be presented with safety attached.

Yet, because products are frequently sold with the promise of meeting deeper needs than they can, we get the simulation of the truth. In fact, we get a simulation of basic human truths that are common to us as extensions of God's creative genius. In a variety of ways, we are promised perfect satisfaction through temporary and inadequate means. This is our SimGospel.

"You're gonna get left behind"

A Wal-Mart commercial shows several high school girls in different back-to-school outfits, obviously thrilled about the new designs. At the close, one girl comments to the effect, "Everyone knows that if you don't keep up with the latest fashions, you're gonna get left behind." Of course, clothing is the tangible item here, but behind this physical representative is a train-sized implication. It not only reminds those who feel left out that they really are, but also reinforces a superficial standard for belonging.

One of the realities of God's design for the individual is acceptance into community. Clothing may promise to meet this intrinsic need, but it cannot actually deliver. With such an ad, peer pressure gains speed, and we end up buying the outfits, thinking that our fundamental need for acceptance can be met with new shorts and T-shirts.

This is the SimGospel's trademark. Through advertising, it attaches a host of Gospel values and truths to tangible

28

items and ideas, and then sells the entire package. It does not stand on its own in reality. It must simulate in a fashionable manner by selling itself through product attachment and by borrowing from real needs of the consumer. Because it does this so appealingly (and often humorously), the charade often goes undetected.

In the Volvo example, we see a trace of the SimGospel rise above the basic premise that their cars are safe. Volvos have been promoted for years in a way that assumes specific responsibility for our protection. This message should concern us regarding the amount of faith we are asked to place in temporary objects. Just as we require acceptance, we also have a basic need for safety. However, I believe there is a subtle misalignment of trust here. To be sure, it is foolish to purposefully buy a car notorious for low protection rates, but are we tempted to provide safety by our own efforts? And at what point will we need to call on God to watch over us, especially if Volvo can do a totally adequate job?

For another example, envision a billboard ad simply showing a Dodge Neon with no catch statement attached. Just a white background with a car in the middle. It is clear that we need transportation, that small cars are better for the environment, and that buying this kind of car even when able to afford a larger one is good stewardship. Besides, this ad only shows a picture of a car, presumably without values attached. However, what effect does consumerism have on the translation of this ad? We always want more, and here is a simple instigator of dissatisfaction with the used car we're currently driving. Coupled with a visual reminder of how to satisfy the craving for more is the SimGospel, teasing us with discontentment and increased desire.

Hopefully, these few examples reveal the importance of delving wisely below the surfaces of images, slogans, and promises. Wisdom will be a decisive guide for navigating through our discoveries of the SimGospel.

In conclusion

Advertising has a very influential yet deceptive voice. Because media come in so many forms, the voice is everywhere, suggesting lifestyles, promising belonging, and disorienting its listeners. Somehow in the middle of this din, we are supposed to discern how to be faithful Christians.

Who are we?

What do we really need?

How should we care for others?

These are essential questions for determining how we should live, even if many Christians raise little concern over how to answer them. On the other hand, advocates of the SimGospel (such as advertisers) answer them via every form of popular media with insight and accuracy by paying considerable attention to our basic human needs. They know us and our needs better than we seem to know ourselves. And their persuasive answers obscure and distort reality in various ways.

Identity, need, and *care* are poorly defined under their influence. These three elements lose the attention they deserve and eventually cease from being seen as interconnected. In other words, we're made to forget that how we see ourselves affects what we think we need, which in turn affects our capacity to care for others. Advertisers hide this critical relationship because they know it would lower our consumption level. Could you imagine an ad saying, "Buy this product, but keep in mind that you only want it because you think you're ugly"?

Holding on to this interconnection is difficult, but when we fail to do it, our perspectives as servants of God become skewed.

In church, I hear that Jesus loves me, and I believe it. I'm told to love my neighbor, and I can tell the story of the Good Samaritan. I learn the importance of being a Christian witness at work, and I might even attend classes on becoming a deacon. Yet all of these elements of teaching are filtered through a Western worldview—a worldview infiltrated by consumerism and excessive autonomy. The truths we claim are often adopted while standing in the middle of the advertising world—a world borrowed, fabricated, and exaggerated for the purpose of selling. If so much of our culture is transmitted via media messages, how much of what we are taught is actually exempt from this influence?

Of course, there is a way to see the difference between the kind of people we want to be and the way we allow ourselves to be subtly shaped by advertising. But it requires that we be in tune with Christ's prophetic message. It requires careful attention and a great measure of discipline to keep up with and tuned to what's going on in popular culture. That is to say, it requires a daily response to Jesus's invitation and commission, which we must not take lightly.

It saddens me to see the effects of the SimGospel on all of us. I hope that this book will help clarify the relationships among *who we are, what we need,* and *how we should care for others.* And I hope that we grasp the importance of bringing these three matters under the healing care of the authentic Gospel. We need the Holy Spirit. We need to pray for increase in our desire to approach this *who, what,* and *how* in a way that unifies us with Christ.

The result will be seeing more of the kingdom come, just as Jesus prayed.

Part I

Who Am I?

2

An Image Bearer

How great is the love the Father has lavished on us,
that we should be called children of God!
And that is what we are!

1 John 3:1

Who does the Gospel say I am?

Samuel Logan Van Eman was born in 1816, in the town of
Canonsburg, Pennsylvania. I am Samuel Logan Van Eman V,
born in the same town, on the same property, almost in the
same house—but 157 years later. That legacy creates a sense
of identity for me in relation to a long line of people who
thought a name was important enough to carry on. Perhaps
they were motivated by pride. Either way, my family line, their

involvement in society, and their commitment to church have contributed to who I am today, and I am grateful.

I am also a child of God. Now, this is something to hang my hat on. This is a statement of identity also, yet it has much deeper implications. It implies origin, moral history, payment and redemption, sanctification, calling, and membership in a heritage that spans 2,000 years. For this, I am eternally grateful.

In Part I, we will look at how the Gospel and SimGospel pertain to us, our neighbors, and ultimately our service to God, but we will start with the concept of identity. Besides the wisdom of scripture, there are many authors who have written about identity from a Christian perspective. I suggest reading Brennan Manning's *Abba's Child*, Henri Nouwen's *Reaching Out*, and Larry Crabb's *Inside Out*. Hopefully, these will enhance your familiarity with such an important and elusive word and add clarity to who we are as human beings.

We are image bearers of God. Little representatives. In some way we are like a product that an advertiser presents with a huge value attached. The difference is that the attachment does not increase our utility value—it *is* our value. We can either misuse that value or give it dignity by accepting it for its worth. Either way, we are forms cast in the mold of God, and we represent him in various ways. According to the book of Genesis and throughout scripture, we learn that dignity, work, love, rest, creativity, relationships, security, play, and so many other attributes belong to God. They are characteristics imparted to us through his love and handiwork, and they not only reflect who God is, but also signify our worth.

Because we are, in a sense, products of the Creator—the ultimate value provider—we have enormous worth and are loved unconditionally by him. Our talents, skin tone, physical stature, strength, emotions, and needs are all held in the care of God's hands. It is here that we receive our true identity. We are God's and we belong to no one else.

Brennan Manning sets up verses from Isaiah by saying:

God speaks to the deepest strata of our souls, into our self-hatred and shame, our narcissism, and takes us through the night into the daylight of His truth: "Do not be afraid, for I have redeemed you; I have called you by your name, you are mine. You are precious in my eyes, because you are honored and I love you . . . the mountains may depart, the hills be shaken, but my love for you will never leave you and my covenant of peace with you will never be shaken" (Isa. 43:1,4; 54:10).[1]

Along with bearing God's image, our identity also includes the aspect of need, which we'll discuss more at length in chapter 3. We *need* to be connected with other people, for we are communal by design. We *need* significance and to know that our lives contribute to others, because we know, subconsciously perhaps, that we have a purpose—a calling. We *need* security and protection, for we are not the source of power; we recognize inadvertently that we are vulnerable to a greater power. Psychologists like Abraham Maslow and Tim Kasser, who will be described shortly, are figures who have given us vocabulary to discuss our needs more definitively.

So identity, at least for the purpose at hand, is a composite of both *image* and *needs*. Physical image and worth, without the presence of needs, make us gods. Conversely, needs without physical image and worth make us apparitions, or simply nonexistent. We are made in God's image, which is beautiful and honorable. And we have needs, which remind us that we are God's creations, dependent on his sustaining power.

Under the Gospel's influence, we know we are sinners, and we trust in a source that actually has the power to redeem. This knowledge humbles us, and our inadequacy bows before the sufficiency of Christ. In theory we believe this, but the SimGospel tells us in a variety of twists that we are something a bit more, something a bit less. Our image is this; our needs are that, it says. It exaggerates trivial points that end up claiming too much attention. It distorts a healthy sense of autonomy, convincing us of a new allegiance. Like Adam and Eve, we begin to hear truth in ways so close to reality that we miss the slight yet significant differences. Because of the subtleties, we remain unaware of being affected and lose accurate sensitivity to God's definition of who we are.

Who does the SimGospel say I am?

Half of the wood he burns in the fire; over it he prepares his meal, he roasts his meat and eats his fill. He also warms himself and says, "Ah! I am warm; I see the fire." From the rest he makes a god, his idol; he bows down to it and worships. He prays to it and says, "Save me; you are my god." They know nothing, they understand nothing; . . . No one stops to think, no one has the knowledge or understanding to say, ". . . Shall I bow down to a block of wood?" (Isa. 44:16–19)

Fool. How is a block of wood or any inanimate object going to save him? I ask the question. Unfortunately, I know the answer from firsthand experience. Although a block of wood may be a poor symbol in modern times, it is still a pertinent sign for the state of humanity, mine included. Living in a sin-filled world makes it very difficult to accurately see the truth of who we are and what we need. As a result, we fashion our own ideas of what may warm the depths of our hearts.

The SimGospel states that we are inadequate. That cannot be refuted. It also says that we need certain fundamental items such as love and security. Again, not out of line. But the question "Who does the SimGospel say I am?" suggests a veering from God's claims on the basis of the word *simulation*. In any simulation, something is lost from the original, and it is deemed incomplete.

The SimGospel veers from a healthy projection of identity when it offers a perfect image, an unattainable image. The more exposure we have to this false projection that correlates beauty with worth, the more we consider it to be real. Slowly, our understanding of beauty and worth, as valued by God, depreciates. Likewise, the SimGospel veers from a healthy projection of identity when it promises to meet our needs through product consumption.

David D'Alessandro, marketing guru and CEO of John Hancock Financial Services knows full well the power of advertising through the concept of branding. His teaching appropriates the SimGospel for the benefit of securing a company's power and permanence in the business world, and his insight reveals how it works.

> If you go into an Ann Taylor store, 9 out of 10 women shopping there will already be dressed alike. Through a reliable combination of fit, styling, and brand message, the company has turned them all into Ann Taylor people. . . . Brands as smart as this turn into cults. The consumer . . . becomes addicted to the experience of buying your products. Entire households commit themselves to the brand. The family understands that if they buy Aunt Tracy an Ann Taylor outfit for Christmas, they are safe. It's her brand, and it gets them off the hook."[2]

And here is the punch line:

> The exchange consumers make with a good brand like this makes perfect sense: The brand offers comfort, trust, convenience, and identity in an excessively complicated world. In return, consumers give the brand their predisposition to buy it over any other brand. This is a very pleasant state of codependency that every brand builder should work to achieve."[3]

From a marketing standpoint, this is a key to success. From a moral standpoint, it poses great danger to our gullible human nature. In SimGospel terms, D'Alessandro's recipe leads to how we often identify ourselves by the hairstyles of *Cosmo* cover girls and by the Abercrombie & Fitch logo branded on our clothing. The SimGospel says that we are not who we are, but rather who and what the cultural icons are.

Bowing to a block of wood speaks volumes to the status we are willing to settle for. Of course it is foolish, but we do it—all of us—to some extent, every day. Wisdom encourages us to start with naming these blocks, or idols, in order to classify them, that is, to put them in their proper place. This requires time and tireless energy, yet even this work is not enough. Wisdom will push us further by demanding that we not only name them, but also deal with their bewitching presence in our lives.

Below is a personal example of how idolatry makes me susceptible to the SimGospel's influence.

Servant to a SimGod

For a number of years, I directed a wilderness program for college students. It was the first of its kind at the university, so it was adopted with enthusiasm. After witnessing a series of successful trips, growing popularity, and several touching student testimonies, I found myself working excessive hours to produce more opportunities for praise. Yet this practice began to have negative effects on my marriage. Eventually, I realized that the affirmations coming from every angle were drawing me further into the work, promising to fulfill a genuine need for significance. I read Henri Nouwen's *Reaching Out* and was caught off guard by his use of the words *prayer* and *illusion* as they pertained to my situation.[4] On the verbal level, my prayers relating to ministry were pious and genuine. But the reality in this situation was that they were misdirected. The program had become saviorlike, a trusted source for fulfillment. And while I did not see it and would not have claimed it, I was practicing illusion.

There was a dangerously subtle difference between attributing honor to God for the ways students and I had received blessing, and seeing the program itself as the provider of my needs. In word, I was praying to the Lord. In action and motive, I was investing my time and heart into the program. Not in the Creator, but rather in the creation. As I said, it was a subtle shift, but the bumps it caused in marriage were clear indicators of something gone awry.

Brennan Manning warns:

> If I must seek an identity outside of myself, then the accumulation of wealth, power, and honors allures me. Or I may find my center of gravity in interpersonal relationships. Ironically, the church itself can stroke the impostor by conferring and withholding honors, offering pride of place based on performance, and creating the illusion of status by rank and pecking order. When belonging to an elite group eclipses the love of God, when I draw life and meaning from any source other than my belovedness, I am spiritually dead. When God gets relegated to second place behind any bauble or trinket, I have swapped the pearl of great price for painted fragments of glass.[5]

The man in the book of Isaiah needed warmth. It was a basic human need, and the wood provided it. He was so thankful *for* it and so impressed by his personal display of talent that he became thankful *to* it. It both sustained and affirmed him, yet it was a swap that cost him dearly.

Because we live in a sinful state, we do not see clearly who we are as image bearers of God. Susceptibility to distorting our identity creates insecurity that we desperately seek to appease. Even if it means finding solace in worshipping a block of wood.

The SimGospel is not new, though. It's just that advertising in an image-based culture makes its illusive promises even more pervasive. In the days of Isaiah, a person might have fashioned an idol using creativity and personal taste and assigned specific meaning to it. Today, she pulls the form from millions of racks and shelves in popularly accepted styles, all branded with logos that have no real meaning. Manning has it: we're still in the business of trading pearls for painted glass.

Enamored of the SimStandard

With modern technology, the number of idols and images produced and digitally enhanced every minute is mindblowing. Just watch one hour of prime-time television and consider how many of them make value statements regarding our identity!

I think of Michelangelo's *David* and of daVinci's *Vitruvian Man* and wonder if there have always been unattainable standards for beauty. Even so, where does this leave the tall and thin, the short and heavy, the old or young and crippled, the bald . . . ? Thousands of makeup and hair-product commercials display models as practically identical: unmarked complexion, straight teeth, a specific waist size. . . . They are always happy, often accompanied by a similar-looking figure of the opposite sex, surrounded by lavish expense, and selling products to me. (I often wonder why such "beautiful" people work so hard and happily for my sake. They don't even know me!)

The models do not look like me, and I am subconsciously aware that this will always be the case. Additionally, it is assumed I need most of the products they represent in order to compensate for some inadequacy or fault, in order for me to look more presentable.

This is not limited to makeup. Cars, beer, phones, computer equipment, lamps, watches, chewing gum, clothing, all get presented to some degree in ways that suggest they will make up for my inadequacies. Bernard McGrane, professor at Chapman University says, "One message you will never hear in advertising is, 'You're o.k. You don't need anything. Just be you.'"[6] Instead, our flaws are highlighted and frowned upon, and in the end, we buy. The question is: Why? Is the product really that tantalizing, or is there something more?

3

A Needs Bearer

What does the Gospel say I need?

Abraham Maslow called them physiological, safety, love, esteem, and self-actualization.[1] Each of these needs, starting with the physiological, must be satisfactorily addressed before we can move to the next one. In other words, we will have no concern with having a roof over our heads if we're starving. And we will have no self-esteem until we're loved.

Needs are what drive families, businesses, consumers, research teams, married couples, beggars, counselors, and students. And they drive us to extreme measures to get them. I've heard that people will drink car oil if they are thirsty enough. We cannot survive without having the basic needs met, and we can't really live without satisfying the higher ones. Whether we follow Maslow's theory or not, we were all designed with a certain set of needs that were intended to be satisfied by the Creator.

In the United States, the poor and rich alike seem to chase after the same dream, propagated by celebrity lifestyles, sexy bodies, and new product lines. This dream promises quick passage through Maslow's hierarchy and we buy into it. We know we have real needs, but the SimGospel preaches so loudly and the message becomes so eloquently entangled with the truth that we end up surrendering to its cheapened form of fulfillment.

Tangible needs

For me, the backpack offers a helpful image here. On a multiday hiking trip with students, it provides a special moment of clarity. It invites me to see the fruitless dependence I put on accumulating goods. Even when I hike an entire week without exposure to civilization, all the physical items I need are in the bag on my back. Furthermore, if the leaders and I are successful in creating an atmosphere of healthy interaction and trust in the group, and if we can develop a relevant, engaging theme during our time together, most of the other basic human requirements can be met without superfluous attention.

Once the physiological needs are met, we can focus on safety needs, such as adequate shelter and being able to locate ourselves on a map. After one or two days, the participants become aware of their relative safety, which allows love needs to be addressed. Depending on the social environment we facilitate, this can happen through activities like Honoring Time, where we sit near the fire and commend each other for service, hard work, or thoughtfulness. From this type of interaction, students gain a sense of significance and recognition from the group. Self-actualization, however, does not occur in a full sense over the short course of a week together. Yet when the intersection of several factors launch a student toward understanding who he is and what he truly needs as God's image bearer, it is indeed a beautiful moment.

Of course, I don't record progress of individuals' movements on Maslow's chart, but growth is quite recognizable, especially when a simple act breaks away from the norm. It thrills me to see the women amazed at their comfort in not having showered for six days. It is great fun to observe the men playing in childlike ways that would never be seen in the classroom or workplace. Walls are dismantled for both sexes. It reminds me of dog who takes off after being released from a chain. Cultural expectations and peer pressure are very restricting for some of these folks.

Moreover, in leaving behind accumulated material goods and the pressure to fill life with nonnecessities, it becomes clear that thirty varieties of soft drinks and fifty feet of shelves stacked four high to hold every conceivable cookie in production is inane. When hunger is felt and especially well earned in the woods, a bowl of butterless, milkless mac and cheese, flavored with bits of uninvited leaf stems, is absolutely delicious. With this clarity, we see the results of being spoiled by a product company: it accurately caters to our picky tastes, and we end up believing that a myriad of options is essential. Yet we are perfectly happy eating no-frills food in the woods because it is all we have. In support of the theory that we are overly catered-to, I can relay countless stories of folks who have attempted to replicate at home a favorite dish from the trip, only to be disappointed by a disaster. They wonder how they ever could have enjoyed it.

What allows this sort of experience? I really think it is a taste of freedom. At the sight of real needs being met in real ways out on the trail, the SimGospel loses its place, and our auxiliary wants lose their grip. While a forty-pound pack can bring sore hips by midday, the confirmation of how much physical and social weight has been left behind in civilization has a profound impact on the mental state of a hiker.

Hiking in a world outside our everyday context jolts us with reality. The amount of stuff we accrue in dorm rooms and closets under the premise of need is embarrassing, if not sinful. Stepping away from "normal" permits us to see how "normal" is defined. As Sut Jhally, a media and culture expert at the University of Massachusetts, says, "We need to get the fish to think about the water."[2]

Intangible needs

In the United States, our idea of normal blurs the difference between need and want. *Needs* are things that I must have. *Wants* are things that I don't need. It might be nice if I had them, but it is not a tragedy if I don't.

Nations such as the United States define need in very different ways than other parts of the world. In a developing country, it may refer to a basic requirement, such as a day's worth of food. In the United States it often refers to *needing* the right shoes for the wedding on Saturday, *needing* to make more money in order to build a two-tier deck, or *needing* to have the radio on the moment we wake up in the morning.

Yet we *need* to use *need* in its proper context.

Psychology professor Tim Kasser suggests that there are "four sets of needs . . . basic to the motivation, functioning, and well-being of all humans: . . . needs for safety, security, and sustenance; for competence, efficacy, and self-esteem; for connectedness; and for autonomy and authenticity."[3] Like Maslow, he gives us terms to work with, handles to grab for discussing these human essentials.

Imagine for a moment that Kasser is correct and that these nine items are the spokes of a wheel. When security, for example, is removed, how do the remaining eight spokes function? What do we do to fix the problem? Now imagine that several are missing and we have no idea how to replace them. Most often, we simply compensate for the lack and endure the displeasure caused by an uneven wheel. (By the way, from a medical standpoint, a neglected ankle injury can cause enough compensation in your gait to injure your knee as well.)

Next, let's imagine this wheel on our Conestoga wagon, traveling through Colorado in the 1830s. We come upon a small roadside stand with a sign that reads "Pioneer Mart." A weathered trader guesses how rattled our kidneys must feel from all the jostling. He shakes his head and comments on how far behind the wagon train we have fallen. As we confirm his statements with a hand massage to our pain-ridden sides and a glance skyward acknowledging the lateness of the day, he pulls out a few spoke replacement packages. Fortunately for us, they are all the right length.

He has a simple version that would cost only one bag of flour in trade and would suffice for our purposes. But he motions toward our rubbing hands and highlights the version with shock absorbers. We buy this latter set out of desire for relief (even though before the old ones broke, we traveled in relative comfort) and are satisfied with their performance. However, within days we realize our three bags of flour traded for the deluxe spokes would have been just enough to reach the next full-sized trading post. As a result, we go hungry for several days. Hopefully, we say, this new need can be met at the next Pioneer Mart.

Lacking, or perceiving to lack, any of Kasser's nine items can lead to foolish and even desperate behavior. This behavior comes when absence of clarity intersects with our desire to satisfy basic human needs. We long for efficacy and connectedness, for authenticity and safety, and the traders at Pioneer Mart somehow know this. They know we don't need the extras, and they know they cannot provide what we really need, but we believe they can, and this codependency ensures a lucrative market for them.

The vacuum

You made us for yourself, O God; we cannot rest until we rest in Thee.

St. Augustine, fifth century

. . . Where is the man [who] can say, "Lo, I have found
On brittle earth a consolation sound"?
. . . What is't in wealth great treasures to obtain?
No, that's but labor, anxious care, and pain.
He heaps up riches, and he heaps up sorrow,
It's his today, but who's his heir tomorrow?
What then? Content in pleasure canst thou find?
More vain than all, that's but to grasp the wind. . . .

Anne Bradstreet, seventeenth century[4]

There is a God-shaped vacuum in the heart of every man
which cannot be filled by any created thing, but only by God
the Creator, made known through Jesus Christ.

Blaise Pascal, seventeenth century

It is impossible, in fact, for man to find true happiness which
he desires naturally in any limited good, because his intelligence at once seizes on this limit, and thus conceives a higher
good, and thus his will naturally desires that higher good.

Fr. Reginald Garrigou-Lagrange, twentieth century[5]

The God-shaped vacuum residing in each of us formed
when Adam and Eve separated themselves from God for the
sake of independence and an unwarranted degree of autonomy.
Of course, we have all made foolish decisions and brought
guilt on ourselves. And like our predecessors, we hide behind
our own fig leaves, knowing that we have done wrong.

If it were only a hole, pressure to fill it would be far weaker
than it is as a vacuum. As a vacuum, there is a drawing power,
a force that acts independently, hindered only by spiritual
filtration and close monitoring of what finds residence there.
This vacuum is attuned to the SimGospel message. It is what
desires the luxury spokes. It is where we feel the absence of
God, and why we seek to fill that absence however we can.

God's desire is to restore us with himself. The power of the
cross to deal with sin is the ultimate source of healing. Torn

emotional fibers caused by our acts of rebellious self-governing respond only to the Great Physician's care. We do need love, security, efficacy, and the rest, for that is how we were created, and nothing is abnormal about this part of our identity. So we must remember that having needs is not a result of sin. Having a God-shaped vacuum is. In one case, dependence is required; in the other, codependence. That is to say, our basic human needs give us opportunity to depend on God's provision—in fact, they require it. But the vacuum initiated by our sinfulness leads us to an unhealthy, codependent relationship with the created order instead of the Creator. The psalmist King David was wise enough to write, "The Lord is my shepherd, I shall not be in want" (Ps. 23:1). In other words, when we trust in the Lord's care and provision, the vacuum loses power.

What does the SimGospel say I need?

"I believe in low-maintenance relationships.
I believe in saving the environment.
I believe in my Civic."
Sounds like the Apostles' Creed for consumers. This commercial for the Honda Civic SI knows that we are in want. The Lord may be a shepherd, but if too many people believe that, then car sales will drop. So Honda writes its own psalm, and it begins by addressing love.

The influence of the SimGospel on our approach to relationships is disheartening. *Stay in it until it gets tough,* we are told. *Live together, but don't commit until you see if you're a good match.* Low-maintenance relationships are easy and painless, but they are fantasy as well. On the other hand, a marriage that endures is a testimony to commitment and faith. It reminds us that relationships aren't disposable like Hondas and milk cartons.

Second, Honda reminds us that at this point in history, saving the environment is cool. I agree, but twenty years ago this might have been a pointless expression in a car commercial. Besides, being environmentally conscious does not require purchasing material goods. It is true that we live in a transient culture, so we require transportation. However, at some point, my Honda will rust away in a junkyard like every other car. By making this purchase, I may harm the environment less than with, say, an SUV, but I am not fooled to think I am actually saving the environment.

Third, because of injected meaning, a vehicle, which exists primarily for transportation, is deemed worthy of my belief system.

Notice, however, that in this ad, the SimGospel does not counteract the message of the Gospel, per se. It undermines it, no doubt, but it does not deny it. It may distort it, but it does not reject it. In fact, the Gospel is its basis. Relationships, environmental responsibility, and faith are Gospel items. If we believe that the good tale of the Gospel is the source for answering who we are, for clarifying the difference between need and want and between real needs and perceived needs, and for guiding us in how we ought to care for others, then there can be no other basis for the SimGospel's message.

So, the SimGospel must borrow as a parasite from its host in order to be recognized by the vacuum within us. That vacuum is God-shaped and can draw only what looks or acts like God, no matter how awfully distorted that may be. Therefore, low-maintenance relationships, saving the environment by buying something that uses the environment, and faith in a material object made of nuts and bolts are items drawn to that hole because in some distorted way, they contain elements of what we are truthfully seeking (i.e., love, obedience as caretakers of God's creation, and faith that won't betray us). The SimGospel must closely simulate the real, so that without careful discernment and shrewd wisdom, it causes us to miss the counterfeit. Obviously, if we did catch it, life would contain less vain and foolish behavior.

Cornelius Plantinga's insight about sin's parasitic behavior is worth stating here again:

> . . . sin is a parasite, an uninvited guest that keeps tapping its host for sustenance. Nothing about sin is its own; all its power, persistence, and plausibility are stolen goods. Sin is not really an entity but a spoiler of entities, not an organism but a leech on organisms. Sin does not build shalom; it vandalizes it. In metaphysical perspective, evil offers no true alternative to good, as if the two were equal and opposite qualities. . . . Good is original, independent, and constructive; evil is derivative, dependent, and destructive. To be successful, evil needs what it hijacks from goodness.[6]

The SimGospel reinforces that we need what we were created to need, and would surely have if it weren't for our fallen condition. It affirms the needs listed by people like Abraham Maslow and Tim Kasser—the same needs we acknowledge by feeling the vacancy within us. Yet it is not enough to ask, "What does the SimGospel say I need?" The question "*How* does it say I need them?" is the counterfeit piece. This is the piece studied so thoroughly by advertisers and presented so delectably through media channels. This is the piece recognized by the spiritual vacuum.

In asking *how*, it is important to look at the methodology employed by the SimGospel to generate such mastery through a simulation.

A Finicky Follower

How does the SimGospel win my allegiance?

Calculation and strategic execution—not randomness—make the SimGospel quite effective. Consumers have particular needs and don't always know how to meet them. But with focus groups, market researchers, sociologists and psychologists, trend analysts and product testers, as well as its enormous budget (over $200 billion in the U.S. annually) and drive to generate profit, advertising seems to know exactly how to meet our needs. It does nothing accidentally, and its promises are superbly tempting. In this chapter, we will look at six highly functioning advertising plans used to win our consumer hearts.

Plan 1: Give meaning to brand names

Brands provide affiliation. They connect us with other people, with a standard of living, with an employer. They disclose our sport and music interests. They are powerful in the sense that they offer identity and meaning, even if superficially. For example, I can imagine what clothing and brand names a middle-aged South Carolina race-car fan might wear. As well, I can envision an educated "soccer mom" from suburbia, a recently graduated intern entering the corporate world, and a one-parent urban teenager who longs to fit in. I might even be able to guess rather closely at some of their values.

Companies have this imagination as well. Yet companies have more power through advertising to actually contribute to image formation. While the following example shows trends to be initiated by consumers, advertising has the power to influence how fashionable an item becomes and what type of meaning it carries in the public realm.

Consider the following cycle:

- DeeDee Gordon is a "cool hunter" who runs a marketing firm called Look-Look.[1] She makes use of diffusion research, the "study of how ideas and innovations spread," and predicts what will be cool before it has even become known.

- Her company of cool hunters ventures into schools and youth hangouts to find those rare individuals who can break popular trends *and* maintain wide acceptance among peers. She knows that these fashion *Innovators* will eventually influence the slightly larger group of *Early Adopters.* Early Adopters are the somewhat daring and relatively influential consumers who follow the wild lead of Innovators. They, in turn, will influence the very large *Majority* groups.[2]

- With a $20,000 entrance fee to Look-Look's website, a company—we'll call it Trendy Clothes—can browse through photographs and descriptions of Innovators submitted by Look-Look staff. Trendy Clothes then buys potentially cool ideas, gambles with success, and markets the product. If it can draw Early Adopters to support the new fashion line, Trendy Clothes will inherit a significant place in the world of cool, and a lofty position in the marketplace (Innovators, by the way, would sooner dig through bins in thrift stores than buy from a Trendy Clothes).

- By the time Mega-marts and the Majority groups (i.e., the general public) enter the scene, Trendy Clothes returns to Look-Look for the latest cool hunter finds. In this way, Trendy Clothes keeps its products fresh for the Early Adopters, who create peer pressure for the Majority. This, in turn, is how Mega-marts do so well financially. They depend on our inadequacies and perceived need to keep up with the higher level of cool emitted by Early Adopters.

- Finally, I shop at Trendy Clothes and wear its logo with pride (whether I am genuinely cool or not). If lucky, my peers will assign value to me as an Early Adopter, and coolness will be determined accordingly. In other words, I can attempt to buy influence and independence, acceptance and status. If my attempt is successful, I will return to Trendy Clothes for more of its products. The company can then rally around their inherited image, ingrain it into the public mind, and capitalize on the establishment of brand loyalty. Here the Trendy Clothes logo ceases from being random and benign to assuming an identity that consumers relate to and want. The brand now has meaning.

Meaning distributors. That's what we are. Advertising companies spend billions of dollars every year on marketing their products to consumers, but this messaging would falter if you and I stopped distributing for free. Rummage through your closet and find every item of clothing with a name brand or company symbol in public view. Now consider that when you don this item, you agree to serve as a walking billboard, by name and by image, witnessing to others what company you support. The irony is that you pay to do it.

Yes, we need clothing. Yes, it is good for clothing to fit and be seasonally appropriate, even enjoyed, but why do companies *not* pay us to advertise? Because we live next door to the Joneses. And if not, we at least hope to in the future. We are haunted by our inadequacies and therefore motivated to act, regardless of financial compensation.

Plan 2: Instill fear

Advertisers propagate a fear of having an abnormal image, of being rejected, or of disclosing failure.

"Will our peer group reject us if they see where we live? Our place is small, the tile is bad in the downstairs bathroom, and we can't afford to remodel the entryway. Maybe they will reject us," we answer, "so let's not have them over."

"Will our co-workers notice that we only have four outfits to rotate through the week, or that we drive a rusty car?"

"Will our children be teased if they don't have an updated computer at home?"

Fear is a powerful inhibitor. It keeps us from living freely. As we will address later, it limits the confidence we have to follow God's intended course of action for us. Using the SimGospel, advertisers create a standard that is impossible to meet, and they highlight our inadequacies when we fail. In other words, they confirm that we should be afraid. When we perceive that others meet the standard more than we do, fear propels us to find significance in order to overcome those inadequacies, even if the pursuit is characterized by futility.

Advertising companies don't need to pay us, for they tell us in the beginning: "Everyone knows that if you don't keep up with the latest fashions, you're gonna get left behind." Unfortunately, we participate in the building of a culture that believes every word of this philosophy.

Plan 3: Exist for the consumer

"Human beings—any one of us, and our species as a whole—are not all-important, not at the center of the world."[3] This was author Bill McKibben's counterstatement to television in 1990. As an experiment, he watched twenty-four hours each of the ninety-three cable stations in Fairfax, Virginia, and then compared it with a one-day retreat in the wilderness. After several months of eight-to-ten-hour days in front of the TV, he realized that he, or anyone else sitting on their own couch, was TV's reason for existence.

He noted how commercials, infomercials, sitcoms, documentaries, interviews, music videos, news, reruns, movies, and all other programs were geared toward him, or you, or me—depending on who is on the couch. We are the main attraction. Though an accurate hypothesis could have been made without watching miles of VHS tape, I find his deduction extremely significant.

By putting us at the center, TV makes us feel important. So important that we become like children who think the sun follows us. Any time we are the object of affection and attention, we react positively toward the person or thing that puts us there.

I spent the evening of my thirtieth birthday in a hardware store, thanks to a surprise party from my wife. For two months Julie made favors, designed games, invited friends, baked extensively, and kept it all a secret.

The actual day was really quite average, as far as birthdays are concerned. Some folks visited the office to wish me well, a few sent thoughtful e-mails, and Julie baked delicious homemade lasagna. She also gave me a thoughtful card, which included an invitation to a seminar on using wood stains. A hardware store was offering the seminar that evening, and I was touched by her willingness to accompany me.

When we entered the store, I asked if she knew the seminar's location or if we should ask at the desk. She said no and mentioned that it was somewhere toward the back of the store. As we rounded the corner, I noticed people wearing party hats at the far end of the aisle. It actually crossed my mind that the employees were having a party and that our seminar would be down a few aisles.

If you have ever been surprised, you know what I experienced next. As soon as it registered, I looked at my wife, who reminded me of Mary Bailey at the end of the film *It's a Wonderful Life*. There she stood, watching her gift open in a celebration of her husband, and I did not know how to respond. Needless to say, it was a joyous occasion, and I spent the next couple of weeks pondering so great a gift. I am important to her, I kept thinking. Very important.

This genuine act of love provided a measure of fullness for my self-esteem and need for connection. These were real needs being met in real ways. The SimGospel recognizes such needs, and it too wants to make me feel important. It will do everything possible to convince me that I am its focus and reason for existence. The difference is that Julie's gift pointed me to the Creator because of true community with her, while the SimGospel points me to myself and then leaves me dangling in emptiness with a hunger for more.

Plan 4: Be subtly honest

In a Winston cigarette ad, four men sit around a table appearing to have a genuine bonding time. Three are conveying camaraderie through highly engaged laughter. The fourth is on the far side, looking between the two whose backs are turned to us. He is smiling at us with intent and warmth, momentarily leaving the conversation to imply, "Yes, this is a good place to be. I want you, consumer, to know that I really enjoy these friends and that I wouldn't want to be anywhere else."

His face, particularly his eyes, and the cigarette he holds are what center our attention. There is a familiar social atmosphere in the ad, but the slogan written below speaks of another dimension: "No fake smiles. No hidden agendas. No bull." These words point to a less familiar aspect of male relationships, which is intimacy. Men certainly have truthful conversations, and these four may be doing just that, but quite often guy talk is referred to as shooting the bull. Deep and meaningful content seems to be more common between females.

The point—and the ad would fail if it were not the point—is that men desire to know each other and to be known by others, to bond with other men in healthy ways. Sadly, the SimGospel connects this need with cigarettes, through the display of men having an intimate time together.

Unfortunately, the ad does not really promise "no fake smiles" when a friendly gathering occurs. Rather, the slogan describes the cigarettes.

This is critical: we, the readers, are the ones making a valuable connection regarding bonding and intimacy. The ad is not.

"No fake smiles. No hidden agendas. No bull" is a slogan specifically describing a 100 percent tobacco cigarette. We know this because the small warning in the top left corner of the ad reads, "No additives in our tobacco does NOT mean a safer cigarette." The reality promised through the slogan therefore is not describing the men, or even health. It is only saying that there are no additives—nothing fake or hidden—in the product. Yet, because we want intimacy, and it seems to exist between the models in the ad, the slogan attaches itself to that need subconsciously. That is our real focus, even though the ad promotes cigarettes whose only reality is that they are 100 percent unhealthy.

Lightbulbs and alcohol and perfumes and expensive cars and gum are all used to unite people in ways we desire and need to be united, yet we know these items will not satisfy our deepest longings. Subtlety in advertising is enough to win our allegiance, however. We are important to advertisers, and being at the center of their universe turns us on and encourages a response.

Plan 5: "Realify" the fantasy world

I never questioned my wife's motives for surprising me with a party. And I never thought the gift was intended for her personal benefit only. But the SimGospel can never be treated in the same way. The SimGospel is never altruistic. Therefore, it is imperative to get behind the scenes and ask what advertisers do to make an ad work.

The thrill of driving fast and hugging the curves of a lonely California shoreline in a sleek car is mesmerizing. Yet most of us know what degree of hard work and/or education is necessary to purchase such a car. Furthermore, we know the time and logistical energy required to arrange for a vacation like this. Recreating this commercial would be quite difficult. First, there is no guarantee of that road being empty. Even if there were, I could not imagine driving like that with my family in the car. Second, we must account for the speed limit and realize how delighted a police officer would be to reprimand our violation.

Pardon me if this spoils the moment. Fantasy can be a good escape so long as it does not disrupt our touch with reality. Even though I would love to be the driver in that commercial, it is only fair to consider the dream it paints. The point is this: while daydreaming is good, buying that car has no power to bring the fantasy to life. In other words, the car will not and cannot recreate that scene.

Similarly, a recent Toyota commercial showed a man racing his car through Los Angeles freeways, intersections, and downtown streets, skidding, spinning, and driving with freedom. If you have ever driven in L.A., you know that those particular roads are never deserted. But that's it: L.A. drivers endure the daily stress of bumper-to-bumper traffic, and the reality is that even if they purchased the Camry, the ride to work on Monday morning would only prove to be more of the same humdrum routine. Yet the desire to be without traffic stress is possibly strong enough to cause them, or any of us who contend with city traffic, to think the Camry would provide just what the commercial shows.

As in the Land of Oz, we believe the Wizard is a mighty figure with power to get us what we most need and want. Only after careful critique do we discover the sham, the man behind the mask, a bumbling old fool trying to provide something that isn't his to provide. For a time, he has the power to draw faith from us, but it is only temporary.

When all of us are all of the time surrounded by all of these dreamy messages, we begin to believe them. They just seem more and more normal. They are everywhere and when something is everywhere and accepted, it becomes normal, even if it was once considered a mere fantasy. Normal is not only the state of comfort where we desire to be, but also the place where our comfort turns on autopilot and we stop thinking in the realm of reality.

For example, people may smoke because it's addictive, or because it's cool, but most often they do it to find relief from a stressful environment. For years, Newport cigarette ads have shown people laughing and playing together. The message is that cigarettes equal good times. Yet when we equate cigarettes, a very unhealthy item, with play, a very healthy item, we normalize the negative effects of cigarettes and also the belief that smoking is synonymous with picnics and love.

Plan 6: Keep the SimBar just out of reach

The SimGospel works overtime at normalizing the abnormal, but every once in a while, a truth-teller from the fantasy world emerges. In the September 2002 edition of *More* magazine, famed actress and model Jamie Lee Curtis presented side-by-side pictures of herself, exposing the difference between typical glamour photos and pre-makeup, pre-touched-up shots. This glimpse of her "not great thighs" and "soft tummy" not only made headlines, but also revealed to the public what we probably know but refuse to acknowledge. In an interview by NBC *Dateline's* Maria Shriver, Curtis said, "I think that the airbrushing, perfect image that we keep perpetuating is fraud. . . . We are an industry built on a lot of subterfuge and fantasy and fakery. . . ."[4] By removing unwanted blemishes and awkward figures, reality is held just beyond our visual reach.

We see millions of advertisements, and most of them contribute to our perception of normal. Inadvertently, we reach for this fabricated state, always propelled by peers, the longing for fulfillment, and feelings of inadequacy. What we discover in our quest is an unattainable standard that accentuates our shortcomings, and we are left with little more than an identity complex.

If every female model, for example, is displayed with a certain standard figure—and she is—then this figure becomes normal. Kilbourne says, "Everywhere you go, when you turn on the TV, or open a magazine, you look at a billboard, and it's essentially the same face, the same body that's defining what's beautiful. We're so surrounded by this image. . . ."[5] And the mirror reminds you, the audience, of exactly where you fall short. For instance, the most stylish clothing is designed for this ideal figure, so if you want the clothes, you must have the body to fit.

A beautiful woman in a white, immaculately decorated home looks directly into the camera (at you) and says, "How can I even think about going out in public when my skin is so dry?" or ". . . when I have such and such complexion problem?" or "off-white teeth?" or "flat hair?" (These commercials vary from product to product, but essentially they keep the same format.) It is an intimate conversation between her and you in her living room. She's not talking to a crowd from a stage. She's just talking to you.

I remember when Bert from *Sesame Street* would turn to the camera at times and address me, just me. He would curiously approach the camera (my TV screen) wondering if I was really there, and then he would treat the thing as if it were a magical portal that connected his world to mine. As a child, this unexpected interaction with Bert changed my level of relationship with the show, even for just that one moment. I often wondered if he could really see me. Even if he couldn't, what a special treat to have his personal attention.

When you hear the beautiful woman ask about dry skin, you think, "If *she* can't go out, and she looks like the officially sanctioned standard, how will *I* ever get out?"

Scrambling subconsciously for an answer, you watch as she lifts the product bottle into view, stating with complete assurance that this will solve her dilemma, and yours. To prove it, she heads out the door with a standard-setting good-looking man, and you are left with a subtle thought: "Where can I get that product?" Because it is subconscious, this little dialogue goes unnoticed. In fact, we most often deny paying attention to it at all.

Kilbourne states, "In addition to selling individual products, advertising . . . teaches us that happiness can be bought, that there are instant solutions to life's complex problems, and that products can fulfill us; can meet our deepest human needs."[6] Advertising is presented in a way that capitalizes on our longings. It exacerbates our fears, driving us to question things we might never have questioned. Bernard McGrane says, "Advertising is designed to generate an inner sense of conflict."[7]

I remember the first time I personally experienced this in a noticeable way. It was on a return trip from the grocery store (an ad mecca itself), and between radio songs a woman seductively asked, "Have you wondered why women aren't noticing you? Have you lost your sex appeal?" After a brief pause, she continued. "If you're going bald, then try this new hair product . . ."

I had recently begun losing my hair, and to my knowledge, it did not bother me. Of course, friends I hadn't seen for years made comments, but this ad came from a stranger. Consider how odd, and awkward, these lines would be in another setting:

Imagine that you are a slightly balding male walking through the park when a seductively dressed woman (a complete stranger) approaches you just as in the ad:

"Have you wondered why women aren't noticing you?" she asks.

You look around for friends who may have set you up with a practical joke, and then struggle for a response to counter her forwardness. Before you gain composure, she steps closer, almost touching you. Slowly, she lifts a bottle from her purse and motions to your thinning hair.

With a glimmer in her eye, she suggests, "Try this new hair product."

Does this seem odd? Why does the encounter in the park seem different from hearing the same words over the radio?

I remember hearing the commercial and being immediately aware of my hair's status. I wondered if it really had an effect on others' perception of me. This seemed unlikely, as I am married and had seen no reason to hide my "condition" before. I was not having a sudden identity crisis, but almost subconsciously, I tried to answer her questions, as we often do when asked something. It occurred to me that the company saw a connection between the questions and the potential success of its product. Otherwise, the script would have been different, and I would not have entertained a possible inadequacy.

Within moments, my mind wandered toward the new wave of men's magazines, which fill enough racks now to warrant their own section at large bookstores. What language, images, and value statements do they promote? What collective effect do they have on the male identity? This, of course, reminded me of women's magazines, which have been doing the same type of harm for decades. Is there a correlation in America between issues related to female body image and the ongoing content that propagates them? Will men face similar problems?

In the grand scheme of things, going bald has no relevance to who I am or to what I need as a human being. God loves me no differently, and my marriage continues to remain unaffected by it, yet the power of such a message, timely and persuasively planted, has the potential for ill effects.

Perhaps you remember a scene from the movie *Tommy Boy*. Richard and Tommy are traveling across the country, attempting to sell enough brake pads to save the late Tom Sr.'s company. As much as this is a comedy, I find the relationship between these two desperate novices to be fascinating. Tommy has a strong sense of who he is because his father embraced him unconditionally, but Richard never experienced this type of love. Consequently, his emptiness shows in many ways, including the toupee he wears. Late in the film he asks Tommy not to disclose his embarrassing secret to a mutual friend. "Don't tell her about my hair!" Richard warns. Tommy looks at him affirmatively and says, "Let it go."[8]

Vanity will drive us to all sorts of foolery, the SimGospel will drive us to all sorts of vanity, need will drive us to all sorts of belief in the SimGospel, and we will end up as fools who keep the cycle flourishing. The problem is that we see saving qualities in products, the same kind of saving qualities associated with a Messiah, specifically the Christ. But Jesus and his Gospel take too long for us. We need a balm for our pain right now, and the SimGospel not only promises but also delivers in the moment, albeit consistently inadequately. It is no surprise that this new "messiah" has a larger and more faithful following than does Christianity.

Success!

Products do provide tangible rewards. Though superficial at times, they are still rewards. Sometimes they come from amassing large amounts of stuff; sometimes from just having the right stuff. Students who have difficulty finding a place in the social crowd often protect themselves from worse harm by dressing like others and acting like others. If there is no foreseeable method to acquire truthful healing, why should they continue to subject themselves to further separation? People want to fit in, and rightfully so. After all, it is a need.

Recently I ate lunch with a new college graduate who had studied hard and scored high, gave the impression to his classmates that he would do well financially with his first job, and sent out his résumé with confidence. After six months, he had not found work and had only twenty-five cents remaining in his bank account. He spoke of how difficult it was to run into ex-classmates who were dumbfounded by his lack of success. He had failed to meet their expectations, and he anguished over this more than having an empty account. The false standards imposed on him by outside forces had won his allegiance, and now he struggled with feelings of inadequacy. He felt average or worse and had nothing tangible to prove otherwise—no company car, no nametag, and no new house.

For years, this former student believed in the façade. He went on faith that if he continued in this superficial manner, he would achieve status, popularity, belonging, power, and significance. These were the intangible returns that held his attention and faith and that were reinforced by the SimGospel's continual presence.

But here, across the lunch table, was a young man who was discovering the Wizard behind the curtain. I watched his countenance change as hindsight illuminated the conditions he had lived under for so long. It was a reality check for him, and it appeared that simply recognizing what SimGospel "membership" meant was a freeing experience. Of course, recognition is only the beginning, but I was thankful to witness this successful step toward healing.

What are the SimGospel's "membership privileges"?

1. Get used to dissatisfaction

We are quite skilled at amassing, or attempting to amass, a great amount of tangible items for the sake of their intangible significance. The SimGospel reminds us that we don't have enough yet, that our neighbor has more, and that our worth will be on hold until we respond with active accumulation.

Large discount stores create knockoff items to make the possessions of the rich available and affordable to the less rich. Mega-marts thrive on the Inadequates wanting to emulate the Adequates, and the Inadequates will not stop this pointless attempt until it is achieved. The sadness lies both in the vanity behind such a pursuit and in the reality that because the Adequate's standard is so high, emulation will never occur. Besides this, the Adequates themselves are dissatisfied. The very rich King Solomon said, "Whoever loves money never has money enough; whoever loves wealth is never satisfied with his income. This too is meaningless. As goods increase, so do those who consume them. And what benefit are they to the owner except to feast his eyes on them?" (Eccles. 5:10–11).

In part, I believe we stress the importance of material goods because they are tangible. With them, we can monitor our own progress, as well as remind others of how we are doing. Ashamedly, Christians are as guilty of overconsumption as the rest, and yet we have no excuse. We herald the scriptures as inspired and trustworthy, and we believe they provide an essential guide for living. We believe they call us to a life of simplicity and stewardship. Yet, even in our Bible study groups and Sunday education classes, we cater to the authority of the

SimGospel and the idea of normal it creates. If this were not true, we would see many more individuals and communities replicating the radical life of Jesus.

When we live and breathe in the middle of this idea of normal, it is very difficult to see well enough to critique it, let alone fight against it. Again, we hear Sut Jhally reminding us about getting the fish to think about the water.

2. You're not good enough, and you don't have enough

Consumerism has a profound effect on our identity. It has a profound effect on the understanding of who we are and what we need as humans created by God.

First, pursuing the *image* that the SimGospel exhibits is a denying of the image we bear as children of God. In chasing after this touched-up version, we are by default claiming to have received less than adequate value from the Creator. Unfortunately, we permit humans and their simulated standards to have more influence in shaping us than we do the One who gave us breath.

Second, if we demand that God meet a particular need and he fails to come through either immediately or in the specific way requested, then we turn elsewhere. In *It's a Wonderful Life,* a run on the bank occurs. The members of George Bailey's savings and loan do not want to take the risk of waiting to get their money in full from George, so they threaten to go to old man Potter's bank to get "fifty cents on the dollar," right now. George sees clearly through the deception and is fortunately able to talk sense into the people. His wife even forfeits their honeymoon money to keep the clients from a foolish and hasty decision.[9]

C. S. Lewis confirms our ignorance by stating:

[Our Lord] finds our desires not too strong, but too weak. We are halfhearted creatures, fooling about with drink and sex and ambition when infinite joy is offered to us, like an

68

ignorant child who wants to go on making mud pies in the slum because he cannot imagine what is meant by the offer of a holiday at the sea. We are far too easily pleased.[10]

When we do not see ourselves in the truest sense, the distortion that fills the void produces what it can, and that is a counterfeit fuel that drives us away from God. Sadly, we most often refuse to invite voices of reason to help sort out our ignorance, or else we act as if they did not exist.

3. You NEED me

When we give into our foolish ignorance, we eventually reap the negative side effects of addiction, dependence, and emptiness. Addiction may be a strong word to use, for not many of us *must* shop today, but consumerism has an addictive edge to it, and we see this when it compels us to make harmful or selfish decisions. The presence of addiction is evident when we intentionally wander from the right course of action so often that we become bound to a new course of action—one that we would abandon if we could.

William H. Willimon, former professor and dean at Duke University, wrote of the typical course of action found in Duke's school of business:

> For several years, students . . . were asked to write a personal strategic plan for the ten-year period after their graduation. . . . With few exceptions, they wanted three things—money, power, and things. . . . Primarily concerned with their careers and the growth of their financial portfolios, their personal plans contained little room for family, intellectual development, spiritual growth, or social responsibility.[11]

Tapping into our self-centered tendencies requires little effort. The students at Duke realized that their wants were attainable, that the track to get there was laid out by the curriculum, and that with some level of faithfulness to the system, their goals would likely be achieved. The yellow brick road lay directly in front of them.

Addiction occurs when we become compelled to follow this road as if it were the only one worth traveling. It occurs when our perceived identity is so entwined in the accumulation of material goods and status that we become bound to its self-inflicted demands. And addiction's partner, dependence, convinces us that beyond the strong desire to stay on this course for selfish reasons, we *need* to stay on it because it feeds us.

> Although they claimed to be wise, they became fools, and exchanged the glory of the immortal God for images. . . . They exchanged the truth of God for a lie, and worshiped and served created things rather than the Creator. . . . Furthermore, since they did not think it worthwhile to retain the knowledge of God, he gave them over to a depraved mind . . . . (Rom. 1:22–23, 25, 28)

We can choose the route of idolatry and be left to the tyrannical whims of depravity. And sometimes we can simply find ourselves there, not remembering having ever made a choice to do so, yet also realizing a tremendous pressure to stay. Idols command our attention, make godlike promises, and eagerly accompany us as we go.

The pursuits and items along this harrowing road are like the shock-absorbing spokes we bought for our wagon. Our choice to acquire more than necessary resulted in dependence on the next salesman for essential items. Our poor decision locked us into specific future decisions in order to stave off hunger. We would *have* to buy at the next "Pioneer Mart." We gave ourselves no choice.

By reflecting on our imaginary wagon journey through Colorado, it is easy to see that dependence provides a great opportunity for market growth. With enough start up customers (like students from the school of business), Pioneer Mart could turn into a small business chain, then a corporation, and, in time, a national powerhouse, providing employment for the wagon train, and selling wagon tarps, saddles, bandanas, and children's moccasins embroidered with the Pioneer Mart logo. Eventually, international expansion could secure enough influence to begin standardizing what kinds of wagons with what kinds of accessories everyone should have.

The motive that causes trouble from the start is simply this: regardless of whether we are wagon owners or corporate executives of Pioneer Mart, we want more than adequate provision. Consumerism holds us because while it seems to add to our lives, it can never fill the void. The God-shaped vacuum remains because material goods were not meant to fill it.

4. You need MORE of me

Consider how Jesus warns the crowd about stuff:

> Someone in the crowd said to him, "Teacher, tell my brother to divide the inheritance with me." Jesus replied . . . "Watch out! Be on your guard against all kinds of greed; [one's] life does not consist in the abundance of . . . possessions." And he told them this parable: "The ground of a certain rich man produced a good crop. He thought to himself, 'What shall I do? I have no place to store my crops.'
>
> "Then he said, 'This is what I'll do. I will tear down my barns and build bigger ones, and there I will store all my grain and my goods. And I'll say to myself, "You have plenty of good things laid up for many years. Take life easy; eat, drink and be merry."' (Luke 12:13–19)

When we moved into our first apartment, Julie and I had few belongings. Though it was a bit tight, we fit into a place with just one closet. Our second apartment was three times the size of the first, and for months the basement accumulated nothing and the closets had space to breathe. Three years later we purchased our first home, and the amount of boxes required to move out of the apartment astonished us. We moved this abundance into a two-story house with a basement, an attic, and a garage, and were thrilled at how much room there was. "Let's keep it simple," we said. But after two years, and three years of having a daughter, shelves began to complain of the load they bore and closets begged for "No Vacancy" signs. Of course, a growing family requires more items and therefore more storage, maintenance, and money, but I am specifically referring to the *surplus* of possessions.

Is there a correlation between amount of space and amount of possessions? Do we say no to accumulation only when we lack the space to store it? Do Americans have poor spatial skills that cause us to put more items in already crowded rooms, thinking that a not-so-crowded corner looks empty?

The problem Julie and I now face is more upkeep and the need to invest additional money and energy into storage every year—purchasing bins for extra clothes, assembling metal shelves in the basement to hold stacked boxes full of knickknacks and surplus picture frames, etc. To-do lists are longer than before. There are more pieces to break and more need for trips to the hardware store. And is our life together any better than before? No, not really. There are more luxuries now, but before we had them we either didn't know they existed or didn't care. Now they require a significant amount of our attention, and depending on the costs involved, we have to work longer and harder to keep them.

In the article, "The Hidden Costs of Too Much Stuff," M. P. Dunleavey shares research from the National Association of Home Builders: "Since 1970, the size of the average house has increased nearly 40% . . . and that's despite an overall decline in family size." Dunleavey's sister-in-law told her, "We all seem to think that the standard of living is celebrities." Dunleavey finds herself in the middle of this mess, pondering over the items she has purchased throughout the years, but forgot she had, and attributes her condition to "SDA, the Senseless Desire to Acquire." She believes that we neither think about our purchasing actions nor restrain ourselves from buying. She is convinced that:

> We succumb to SDA and squander money on temporary pleasures without thinking about what, really, we're investing our money in—and the fact that our money would almost certainly be better employed elsewhere. . . . Whether it's eating on the run or buying shoes on impulse, instant gratification rules the day.[12]

Immediately after the tragedies of September 11, 2001, President Bush encouraged America to buy more stuff. Keep the economy alive. Have faith that by spending, we can get through this catastrophe. Our money says, "In God We Trust." But it wasn't a church that was attacked—at least not a typical church. It is obvious that targeting something closer to our hearts would have a more crippling effect. The two towering icons, which stood proudly in Manhattan's financial district, were religious symbols. They represented our center of devotion, the object of our attention and worship. Seeking for answers and comfort, we listened to America's pastoral leader, who proclaimed clearly that day the SimGospel's message of salvation: buy more stuff.

These words were intended to provide hope in the wake of a tragedy. I'm not ignorant of their importance for stimulating the economy, but what do we do with scriptures such as Psalm 33:12–20? "Blessed is the nation whose God is the Lord. . . . No king is saved by the size of his army. . . . A horse is a vain hope for deliverance, despite all its great strength it cannot save. . . . We wait in hope for the Lord; he is our help and our shield." Even in tragedy, we not only have a Senseless Desire to Acquire, but we are ordered to obey it by the most authoritative voice in America.

Wisdom from a simple Leader

I could easily chart my time and energy over the last few years to show the relationship between free time, possessions, and work. The results would concern me. They should. Not only have I been moving away from a life characterized by elements of simplicity, but I have invested myself in things that Christ warned about: "Do not store up for yourselves treasures on earth, where moth and rust destroy" (Matt. 6:19).

Why the warning from Jesus? Is it because a microwave oven is evil? Have garage door openers and DVD players been picked from the tree of forbidden fruit? A few passages later Jesus points behind the products: "For where your treasure is, there your heart will be also" (Matt. 6:21).

Jesus had the kind of eyes that could see through the facade immediately. He knew it was there, which allowed him to reveal it to others by going straight to the heart of the matter. Possessions were not denounced—the faith in possessions was. Of course, this does not give me license to splurge so long as I promise to keep my greed in check. I know that through the din of voices vying for my attention, it is incredibly difficult to discern what is true. So I caution myself from making such a promise. My heart must be guarded against easily attained fulfillment, for I know from experience that I lack strength to sit in luxury without slumping into vanity.

So, what about he who dies with the most toys? Let him. It's a race I don't want to enter.

Recap

The SimGospel enters the room like a nurse with a medium dose of painkiller. She has enough to ease our immediate discomfort, but only enough so that we want more in a few short hours. We lie in bed, dependent on her to provide what we cannot provide for ourselves, and we believe so much in her air of proficiency that even though she did not seem to help us much yesterday, we are convinced that her care will be sufficient today.

When using first aid in the wilderness, it is important not to give pain relief medication to a patient before the paramedics arrive. It can hide critical information used to determine the severity of the injury. It also obscures the best method for treatment. What the patient wants is relief, and she wants it now. But without the ability to give an accurate description, long-term healing can be jeopardized.

The SimGospel promises to care for us in ways we need, and it presents solutions that offer immediate and acute results. Yet, while the diagnosis may be accurate, the application is too general for us to realize as consumers that the injection is insufficient.

Buying stuff is an injection often accompanied by a short period of elation. However, we soon recognize that lack is still there, and pressure to meet the standards of Normal remains. Our failure to see God as the qualified caregiver decreases our openness for deep healing to occur. Instead, we permit the SimGospel to care for us again today because we are forever seduced by its eye-candy promises. The cycle continues, and we become faithful people to a merciless and phony god.

When we know that material goods will not fill our deepest desires but pursue them anyway, we neglect to care adequately for ourselves. When we deliberately gather up treasures on earth, we neglect God's care for us. When we fail to recognize that we are made in the image of God, we neglect true dignity, beauty, and worth.

In Part I, we discussed the SimGospel's empty promises and a few ways it attempts to carry them out. We named methods employed to spread its message, looked at how they function, and briefly considered what sort of accomplice we play. Furthermore, we discussed the negative side effects that result from our infatuation with the SimGospel's idea of normal. With regard to the Gospel, we began to tell of the marvelous ways we are loved, and we considered how image and need might by viewed from a biblical perspective. In all of this, the primary focus was on us.

We must now turn from attention to self to a focus on others.

Our foundation in Christ and the guidance of the Spirit will serve as a collective basis for understanding this next section. It will offer the necessary wisdom to show how we should care for others as people who are made in the image of God.

Part II

Who Is My Neighbor?

5

An Image Bearer Next Door

I am not alone. The fact that I have children or siblings, or that I work for an employer, study under professors, rely on the mail carrier, or receive phone calls proves that I am not alone. Even a hermit has parents. In other words, I have contact with others; I influence and others influence me. This makes us all neighbors. But there is a problem I should address before going further with the question "Who is my neighbor?" Consider the following.

God is at the center of all existence. In Exodus 20:4–5, he commands that we not worship any other gods or idols before him. He wants and deserves all glory, for he is the source, and therefore all honor should return to him. The apostle Paul confirms this when he says, "For from him and to him and through him are all things" (Rom. 11:36).

John Piper suggests that we often think of God as acting fully on *our* behalf, such as with Jesus's redemptive work on the cross, or with the creation of human beings. It is true that we are rescued by his gracious hand, and that we benefit incredibly from his care, but numerous verses imply that these are for *his* behalf.[1] As it is written in Isaiah 48:10–11: "See, I have refined you, though not as silver; I have tested you in the furnace of affliction. For my own sake, for my own sake, I do this. How can I let myself be defamed? I will not yield my glory to another." God is in relationship *with* me, but God does not exist *for* me, and it would be ridiculous to think otherwise.

It sounds awkward, but we could say that God is utterly self-centered. And we would be correct in this, for God has every right to be so. Remember that he is the source, and therefore he does not sin when he worships himself. (It is rather difficult to think of how this attribute pertains to God from within a framework of sin.) For example, Christ's work on the cross certainly redeems us, but only so that our wholeness will point others back to God. He uses wholeness and health to shine in a sinful world of broken pieces and sickness, and these glimpses of heaven reveal that One greater than us is responsible for the goodness we see. The result is worship of God, initiated by God himself.

We, on the other hand, are only representatives of the source. Therefore, when we worship ourselves, or other idols, we sin. We sin because we assume a position that is not rightfully, not possibly ours. Because we consistently desire to be at the center of the universe, the offer to be like God is terribly enticing. It was for Adam and Eve; it is for us in the twenty-first century. Herein lies the problem: the idea of *neighbor,* or otherness, has little substance, both in our thinking and, especially, in our practice. The "me first" syndrome threatens and fractures wholeness in relation to other human beings. And yet, we are called to community and to love others.

Self-centered and communal. The paradox is numbing, but ever present. Looking to the Gospel for clarity and taking time to expose the SimGospel for its heresy are critical in this predicament—especially if we are to find any success in renouncing ourselves for the sake of God and others.

Who does the Gospel say is my neighbor?

A softball coach. An enemy. A lover. A child molester and a leukemia patient. A state senator with controversial views and a caseworker in the welfare office—even the one who hustles her dependent customers through like cattle. A matron of honor. A thoughtful sister. A New York City cab driver. A beggar.

A self-absorbed movie star. An eighth-grade bully. A confidante. A car salesman with a glimmer in his bogus smile and dollar signs in his handshake. A best friend, a mother, and a neighborhood boy who tramples flowers. A valedictorian. A messy roommate. A city ordinance officer and a bulimic girlfriend.

If I live at 1313 Mockingbird Lane, then my neighbor is surely at 1311, or 1315, or 1312 Mockingbird Lane. If I live on the east side of town, then my neighbor is also on the west side of town. If I live in the state of Pennsylvania, then my neighbor is in Texas or Lithuania!

Neighbor is anyone other than myself, including some with grave needs and others with no unusual needs. Some may have beautiful gifts to offer, and others only a pittance. All neighbors, however, require some level of care. Perhaps you can see the difficulty caused by our self-centeredness. It is hard to care for neighbors who require sacrifice, because servanthood is expensive in one way or another. But being in community with others is the bedrock of society and culture. To isolate ourselves with the spirit of individualism is to forget who we are.

As I have said, being made in the image of God makes each of us representations of the One whose image we bear. We are not the source, but rather a representation of the source, which implies dependence, and dependence implies relationship to another—specifically, to God. Understanding that God is trinitarian leads us to understand that one of the fundamental realities of our image bearing is that we are not without relationship. Consider the following comments by theologian Richard Gula:

> . . . God in whose image we are made is a community of persons radically equal to each other while absolutely mutual in self-giving and receiving.[2]
>
> The Trinitarian vision sees that no one exists by oneself, but only in relationship to others. To be is to be in relationship. The individual and the community co-exist. Humanity and relatedness are proportional so that the deeper one's participation in relationships is, the more human one becomes. . . . [C]ommunity is necessary to grow in God's image.[3]

Because we do not live outside of community, we must consider the significance of others. In the Gospel of Luke, Jesus told an expert in the law, "Love your neighbor as yourself" (Luke 10:27). The man asked, "And who is my neighbor?" (Luke 10:29). From this brief exchange comes the famous story of the Good Samaritan, a smashing example of the stretching hospitality that requires selfless care.

The Jew who was robbed and left for dead received no compassion from his actual neighbors. This left room for surprise in Jesus's parable. Describing the victim's provider as a Samaritan elicited a clear response from the Jewish crowd, for if this kind of unwelcomed foreigner could offer what the expected neighbors could not, what was Jesus saying to the expert in the law?

In Luke 6, Jesus admonishes us: "Love your enemies, do good to those who hate you, bless those who curse you, pray for those who mistreat you. . . . Do to others as you would have them do to you" (vv. 27–31). Neighbors are family members and best friends, but more challengingly, they are those who may not thank us, those who are different from us, those who are poorer than us. In *Making Room: Recovering Hospitality as a Christian Tradition,* Christine D. Pohl reminds us:

> Just as God would welcome all to the feast in the Kingdom of God, so earthly hosts ought to open their tables to those in need and without ability [or intention] to repay the kindness. In God's economy, all would then experience blessing. The character of God's hospitality frames appropriate earthly behavior.[4]

But what happens when God's principles are left out of the equation? Who do others become to us?

The SimGospel is quite capable of telling us.

Who does the SimGospel say is my neighbor?

The SimGospel makes many statements about our relationships with and treatment of others. It spends its energy focusing on me, but while doing that it makes spoken and unspoken implications about others. Obviously, this is detrimental to communal health.

In Part I, I asked the question, "How does the SimGospel win my allegiance?" Then I answered it with descriptions of common advertising practices that affect you and me (imagine that we are both targets of the SimGospel's arrows). Yet the SimGospel's general scheming isn't limited to this one-way damage—from it to me and you. Rather, it also muddles my ability to clearly observe and discern scripture regarding treatment of you. In other words, it also causes damage from me to you. (Imagine that I now turn and shoot arrows at you also. Mine are different from the SimGospel's, but they are still shot as a form of attack.)

When I am the fixed point of an advertiser's gaze, for example, a false superiority promotes me above you and elevates my needs above yours. When encouraged to have the better lawn mower, I am pressed to earn more in order to have more than you do. Sadly, while I already have one good mower and now look for an upgrade, a needy neighbor within reaching distance has none at all.

Thoughtful would be to give my old model to this neighbor in need. A bit more *sacrificial* would be to buy the upgrade for me and another of the same for her. *Radical* would be to buy the upgrade for her and keep the old one for myself, even at the expense of taking second place to you, the mulching and self-propelled competitor next door. Unfortunately, we frequently neglect all three of these.

The SimGospel's mesmerizing influence on redefining "neighbor" is done by capitalizing on our human frailties—pride, envy, apathy, etc.—and then encouraging those weaknesses to be the basis for understanding, or misunderstanding, others.

I'm the target audience, and you are . . . ?

I have watched a lot of television in my lifetime. And in reflecting on commercials especially, I find it hard to recall substantial moral content regarding treatment of neighbors. In chapter 4, I wrote of Bill McKibben's cable television experiment.[5] If his theory is true—that *I* am television's object of affection—then *neighbor* has very little significance according to the SimGospel, at least when we think of neighbor as a recipient of our care and love.

According to the SimGospel, I am the target audience. I am all that matters. I am the whole reason for its being, the power by which it runs, and the motive for such beautiful people to spend extensive time and energy presenting products. My self-centeredness, already quite adequate if you will, now takes on epic proportions as I receive undivided attention from these

84

beautiful people. These are people I long to emulate; people assumably worthy of my faithful following; strangers whose names I wear on my shirt and hat, whose posters make it to teenager bedroom walls, and who are recognized on a first-name basis by the general public. What better relationship could I ask for? Those I adore most, centering their existence on me. It creates a perfect working union!

The SimGospel's treatment of me, though, eventually has the effect of building fences and making me codependent. The fences grow as I come to believe that advertising is correct in naming me as the focal point. Should this kingly position be threatened, hostility will most likely arise against you, my neighbor. And codependence occurs as I invest in this illusion. It is an abusive relationship in which the SimGospel makes promises, I believe and invest, and the SimGospel reneges. The cycle repeats itself, and in this process, I lose the ability to care for you adequately.

Remember, not all advertising is harmful to my relationships with others. But I am referring to the most common form that we see during sitcoms, before movie trailers at the theater, on countless pages of popular magazines, during countdowns on radio stations, throughout the mall, on billboards as we drive, and plastered on the sides of city transit buses. In most cases, these venues result in us seeing our neighbor as a *standard*, a *competitor*, or a *nonentity*.

She is a *standard* because she signifies an ideal that cannot be attained. He is a *competitor* because I am full of pride and encouraged to fight for higher recognition and status. And often, she is seen as a *nonentity* while the SimGospel focuses its utmost attention on me and encourages my apathy.

Neighbor as a standard

In chapter 4, "Plan 6: Keep the SimBar just out of reach," I said that advertising sets models and lifestyles on a fabricated plane—just out of our reach. This unachievable standard manipulates through two goals. The first is to generate dissatisfaction with our current situation. The second is to promise perfect solutions.

Unless it pertains to one of our basic human needs such as hunger, the phrase "We don't have enough" is bunk. Yet commercials, like those for beauty products, thrive on this. They make this a comparative statement based on what others *do* have, whether looks, money, or popularity. We say and think this statement because we are continuously reminded of how we do not look and what we do not have. Inadequacy permeates the ad world, causing us to think that neither we nor our belongings are good enough. Consider the two-part scheme of infomercials. On one hand, infomercials expose the faults of our knives and screwdrivers, but, more important, they use these faults to state that people with average, outdated lifestyles are also faulty. Who wants to be like the man who tries to use a screwdriver in the dark but can't because his "leading brand" didn't come with a built-in, adjustable light (available for $19.99 if you call in the next two minutes)? After dramatizing his plight by dropping the tool, losing the screw, and nearly falling off of the ladder, he makes a fool of himself in an overexaggerated, disgusted way, showing that this is no way to live.

Dissatisfaction is the ad world's tactic for creating "new" needs. And so, the second goal of standard setting is to provide perfect solutions for these new needs: if you want to reach the standard, you must avoid this, buy that, dress like him, and flaunt like her. Or else you, too, will be frustrated with this below-standard modus operandi. Keeping the standard just beyond our reach makes it profitable, effective, and unattainable.

However, if I can keep merely one step ahead of you, even if I can't reach the standard, it will be good enough.

Neighbor as competitor

Competition is everywhere. Babies compete for toys. Teenagers compete for independence. Adults compete for positions and affirmation. In many situations, competition is invigorating and leads to healthy growth, such as between teams or neighboring restaurants. However, the SimGospel seems to have no intention of fostering healthy attributes. In order to make significant profit, advertising must create a distorted form of competition between parties. I say distorted because reasonable goals are lacking when the SimGospel determines the rules of play. In this game, we are urged to compete against our neighbor for the purpose of getting ahead, securing worth for ourselves, or creating envy. We are not pushed to reach for the greater good of all.

Consider the following magazine ad.

A centerfold spread reveals the deluxe, leather interior of a new Nissan Maxima. The highlighted text in the top left corner reads, "One seat for exhilaration. Three seats for petty jealousy, resentful mumbling and wishful thinking." Is this a beneficial reason to buy a car? Does this promote friendship and exhibit a healthy form of competition?

Competition becomes problematic when power is the goal. Power teases men and women with the ability to control, because control translates into significance. We know inferiority lacks all three, so it is often difficult for us to be lorded over, whether by a boss or simply the driver's seat of a new car. Yet, when significance is gained through a grounded identity in Christ, we do not crave power, whether we have it or not.

Neighbor as nonentity

Beer commercials are memorable. They are also highly guilty of distorting the way we see others. We watch the images, listen to the messages, and often miss very important connections. They are often driven by sexual content, and alcohol is frequently portrayed as the ticket to intimacy—or at least to a one-night stand. One sickening ad, in particular, shows a bottle of alcohol underlined by the words "Liquid panty remover."

87

According to the Center for Substance Abuse Prevention, "one in four teenagers will experience sexual or nonsexual abuse by the time they finish college or turn 21." And "more than 60 percent of sexual assaults involve alcohol."[6] Take a moment to make the statistical connection.

When men, especially, are bombarded with and believe the equation that beer leads to romance and to getting the idealized woman, the SimGospel is performing at its finest. The following well-known TV commercial will help us see how the SimGospel can turn our neighbors into *nonentities*.

Two women are dressed well and sitting in an outdoor café. We enter the scene as they begin to argue whether their Miller Lite beer "tastes great" or is "less filling," and a risqué battle ensues.

Within moments, they stand like cowboys in a saloon, knocking over chairs and challenging each other to a duel. They begin to claw at each other and pull hair. As they continue yelling "Tastes great!" and "Less filling!" clothing is ripped off. They fall into a nearby pool and end up in bikinis, still going at it for most of the commercial.

The ad is strongly sexual, and many camera shots intentionally highlight their physical attributes. But just before the ad gets too revealing (I say *too* revealing, but isn't that horribly relative?), we are transported to a bar, only to realize that we have been participating in the fantasy of two beer-drinking men.

"Now, that would make a great commercial!" the first one exclaims. And without hesitation, the second replies, "Who wouldn't want to watch that?!" The camera immediately pans to the other side of the bar table, where we see the dreamers' actual girlfriends staring at them in disbelief.

Now, it is possible that they have no clue what their boyfriends were just doing, but that is irrelevant. The fact is *you* and *I* make the visual connection.

Without saying a word to the girlfriends, the men re-enter their fantasy. The voluptuous models are still barely clad, but now they are more playfully wrestling in a mud pit. We never return to the bar, and the commercial ends with a reminder that Miller Lite is the sponsor.

Seeing this ad for the first time made me wonder a few things:

1. How does something like this get approved?
2. What woman in her right mind would audition?
3. What caliber of relationships, with regard to dignity and self-worth, do the guys have? (I guessed what my wife's response would be if I were one of them.)
4. Does anyone (particularly female viewers) care about the messages it conveys?

Ironically, alcohol is the inanimate cause for the girlfriends to be ignored and for the fantasy girls to be declothed. It supersedes the value of all four women, and leaves them as mere physical objects to be rejected or desired.

While the fantasy girls are the main attraction, the girlfriends are used only to reinforce the ad. They certainly play a lesser role, but they are equally mistreated: dressed plainly, given no speaking parts, introduced last among the characters, and left behind without acknowledgment. In essence they are told, "Oh, we forgot you were sitting there. Anyways, where were we? Oh yeah, the mud pit!" They are like extras on a film set: background, unnamed, and quickly forgotten.

What prospects do these relationships in the bar have? What is the role of value and dignity? Where are intimacy and trust and the reminder of being made in the image of God? Nowhere. Nonentities are never given these things, and that's exactly what the SimGospel wants. These elements take too long to acquire, and the SimGospel is sharpest when it can thrive in the present. It must keep us seeking pleasure in the moment, because that is when it delivers.

And pleasure it provides. The behavior and physique of the fantasy girls are what sells for Miller Lite, and they obviously set a standard that is not met by the girlfriends at the table. Otherwise, the girlfriends would be doing the imaginary wrestling, no? Here the fantasy girls represent the standard for women, the typical image setter. They appear before millions of female viewers, reminding all of them what men dream about (these two are the objects of male fantasies, after all). They have the ideal physical characteristics, which serve as attention magnets, but that is all they have.

As the standard, they aren't even real to us—only fabricated projections of beauty. Even if they were real, they are stripped of all other valuable characteristics, particularly intellect and modesty. What we remember are body parts, an asinine debate, and cat fighting. Collectively, they are the ideal, with enough power and influence to remind women of their physical "inadequacies," and yet we couldn't care less about them. They, like the actual girlfriends, end up as nonentities.

Because none of the four in the commercial is treated in a respectful way either by Miller Lite or by us, they are automatically given a lower value. We intentionally or unintentionally redefine worth despite the price God has put on them, and in doing this, we allow distortion to remake people in our own eyes. Perhaps we should consider what guilt the two men incur.

There are millions of Internet sites dedicated to pornography and dozens of men's magazines designed to stimulate male fantasy life. Surrounded by images and messages that make women into nonentities, how difficult do you think it is for a man to imagine a woman as a neighbor to love and to treat with care? How is such exposure going to permit men to view women with dignity, when most of the half-naked models we see in advertising are representing products to buy?

Women are tools of the advertising trade. They are used and abused to provide pleasure without the long road to intimacy, and capitalized on to provide products for consumption. Ads for water, appliances, cars, vacations, medication, financial services, cosmetics, clothing, eyeglasses, alcohol, tobacco, computers, TV shows, sports equipment, furniture, picture frames, pet food, phone books, hiking boots, seminars, cameras, role-playing games, fitness centers, automobile tires, cereal, soft drinks, and thousands more items are carried by the bodies of women. She, this equal of males, sadly loses her God-given worth and becomes a product herself.

When images of women in ads become normal, we can easily forget that she is really a life-bearing representative of God. She has been normalized for so long that it is hardly disturbing. I have spoken with students about this type of advertising and heard many of them say, "It's the model's right to be there. At least she is being honored for her beauty."

These are normal responses to a much-normalized abnormality. Of course it's the model's right. But rights have nothing to do with whether the act is moral or not. On the outermost surface, I might consider that a model is being honored for physical beauty, but when she is dissected into thighs and lips and necklines and breasts, and all nonphysical faculties are silenced, and when her disclosed body and erotic motions are selling America Online to computer users, the veil of dignity thins and I can no longer justify that she is being honored in any decent way.

In reality, the product is the honoree, and no matter its quality or significance, it is deemed worthy by the supporting beauty of a woman. The product becomes the noun and she is demoted to adjective status. So long as she honors the car tires or the soft drink, I am visibly told that she ranks just below the product. In other words, while she is being objectified, she is not the object of the advertisement, but only the modifier. I do not take conscious notice of this, but, nonetheless, it is the image that I and millions of others are exposed to daily.

Does it have a cumulative effect? Jean Kilbourne thinks it does:

> Everyone in America feels personally exempt from the influences of advertising. So wherever I go, what I hear more than anything else is, "I don't pay attention to ads. I don't look at them. I just tune them out. They don't have any effect on me. I hear this most often from young men wearing Budweiser caps.[7]

A woman's insight

In *Eve's Revenge: Women and a Spirituality of the Body,* Lilian Calles Barger offers very helpful insight regarding beauty and the problem it has encountered in our culture:

> At a time when women of many classes and races have greater economic, political, and social access, the camera that ought to reflect the multiplicity of ways women are women has instead narrowed the concept of beauty and made it more demanding. . . . [This] means we are constantly bombarded by concrete and codified images of beauty that assault the senses.[8]

Barger supposes that when an earlier, text-based culture described beauty, any woman could imagine herself to be the Beloved of God. But images defined on the cover of *Cosmopolitan* magazine retard the imagination today, and women quickly become aware of a *standard* for beauty. An "image-laden culture leaves little room for the romantic imagination. By emptying beauty of its ability to point us toward the good . . . mass-media culture ironically manages to be antibeauty," she says.[9] Her despair is shown when she remarks, "With no alternative place on which to fix our own gaze, the cultural images of beauty become for us an idol and begin to fulfill a spiritual role."[10]

The difficult task

Too often, neighbors are people I end up envying, competing against, or ignoring. And the media-saturated world around me is inundated with messages that hide and distort the Gospel. For these reasons, I desperately need guidance.

Jesus says that I must love my neighbors, but his voice is often heard as one of the many. Regardless, it is still there. If I am to move from consumption to engagement, I must turn from self-centeredness and face the realities of living with neighbors. Indeed, it is a difficult challenge. Writer Ann Hagmann says, "People are not means to an end. Each person has an intrinsic worth equal to that of every other person in the sight of God, simply by virtue of possessing the gift of life."[11]

Hagmann suggests that even focusing on others can be done poorly if we are not careful to listen to Jesus. For example, she says that we often use productivity as a measuring stick for worth: "From the human perspective, a business executive has more worth than a mentally handicapped adult."[12] I am saddened by my own guilty response to this statement. Meanwhile, I understand and support her previous comment that others have intrinsic worth in the sight of God. I concur that all humans are of equal worth, but at the same time, I am a victim of a mania for productivity.

Isn't this how we treat people every day? Don't we praise those who accomplish much? Don't we scorn the abusers of welfare and not just their abuse of the welfare system? Haven't we removed dignity from the elderly due to their lack of productivity? Don't we steal worth from the recovering addict because she exacts a large amount of financial support from the state?

Yet these are our neighbors, and Christ showed no distinction between them. In fact, he emphasized the needs of the least productive and called his disciples to care for the poor, the hungry, and the fatherless. My sinfulness results in asking the following questions regarding worth: "God loves *her* as

93

much as he loves *me*?!" and, equally saddening, "God loves me *only* as much as he loves *her*?!"

With this selfish assumption, I neglect to see that she bears the same image as me. I fail to remember that "all have sinned and fall short of the glory of God" (Rom. 3:23), which renders me equal to her regarding the need for a Savior. As well, I forget that all "are justified freely by his grace through the redemption that came by Christ Jesus" (Rom. 3:24), which proclaims that I am just as unable to get to the Savior on my own. Before the throne of God, I am equally in need of his mercy, and equally granted pardon should I accept it.

The apostle Paul is aware that humans have a tendency to regress. Therefore, he admonishes the church in Rome in a simple, yet challenging manner, regarding neighbors: "The commandments, 'Do not commit adultery,' 'Do not murder,' 'Do not steal,' 'Do not covet,' and whatever other commandment there may be, are summed up in this one rule: 'Love your neighbor as yourself' " (Rom. 13:9).

I believe this verse has more value to us than we may think. I think other passages, like those of the Good Samaritan, also offer more guidance than we suspect. They are powerful tools against becoming the center of attention and accepting individual self-aggrandizement as the target audience. But how do I love my neighbor if I don't know what she needs? How could the Good Samaritan care for his neighbor if he didn't know what he needed? I mean, it was one thing for him to see the wounded man as valuable enough to approach; in this, he shamed the other travelers. But, it was knowing what the man needed, and then responding to those needs, that did the rescuing.

We have looked carefully at how self is heralded as the zenith of advertising. And we have considered the effects this has on how we often see our neighbors. In order to move from knowledge to action, from consumption to engagement, we must ask, "What does my neighbor need?"

6

A Needs Bearer Next Door

How should I care for my neighbor?

"For I was *hungry* and you volunteered with Meals on Wheels, embraced a teenager who was starving for attention, and went to the grocery store for a single mother of four children.

"I was *thirsty* and you did research for an irrigation project in India, donated to a Bible translation ministry, and took quicker showers in the morning.

"I was a *stranger* and you provided an encouraging word to the grocery store cashier, called for a towtruck to pick up a stranded driver, and lent an attentive ear to a grieving co-worker.

"I *needed clothes* and you dropped off bags of hand-me-downs (plus a few new items) to the City Mission, surprised

95

the women's shelter with Christmas gifts, and handed your coat to a homeless man.

"I was *sick* and you threw a tea party for a hospital patient, served as a designated driver, and took soup to neighbors with the flu.

"I was *in prison* and you counseled a friend through his alcohol addiction, sang for chapel at the county jail, and asked state governors for reform.

"I tell you the truth, whatever you did for one of the least of these brothers of mine, you did for me" (Matt. 25:35–40, paraphrase).

Caring for others has been central to God's will since the creation of humankind. It is our calling. Starting in the Old Testament, the people were given rules of conduct that, when followed, would result in loving treatment of others. Often, these principles were very radical to our selfish ways. The jubilee concept in Leviticus, for instance, called for land to be returned to the poor and debts to be forgiven. MasterCard never would have survived in that climate.

The book of Proverbs listed instructions for how to live selflessly and honorably regarding others. The prophet Ezekiel addressed Israel's religious leaders—its shepherds—and confronted their lack of care for the flock.

In the New Testament, Jesus took these rules to another level by making them tangible. He physically embodied this call and set an unprecedented example for how to care. With his disciples hardly ready, he sent them into the world to replicate his model by living the Gospel message. The church began and was established on the same governing principle: love your neighbor as yourself. To this end, Paul encouraged the church, through Timothy and others, to live a life of integrity and holiness. He diligently called all believers to live in the likeness of Christ.

The Holy Spirit has continued to work through believers for the past nineteen or so centuries, and today our pastors and priests ask us on any given Sunday, "What does your neighbor need?"

A Christian witness

When we respond to this general call of sharing God's love with others, it becomes known as our witness. When we attend to the needs of others, we serve as a witness for Christ's love, even centuries after his actual ministry. It is like a thread of holy care that weaves back through countless saints and laypeople to conversations like the one about the Good Samaritan.

Reaching out can be rather quite challenging, though, if we are not careful to avoid the SimGospel's influence. With self staged at the center, it is difficult to see others in their need and to know how to serve them. Author and professor Steve Garber contemplates one of these specific difficulties as it applies to contemporary culture:

> We are to learn to read the Word and the world, at the very same time. How is it possible? How do we, like the apostle Paul, walk through the marketplace of ideas and images of our day, holding onto the integrity of the gospel, and at the same time engage in "Mars Hill moments" with our family and friends, in our society and the wider world?[1]

Unlike Paul, we live in an advertisement-saturated society. Yet the Areopagus Model is just as applicable. Caring for our neighbors today is certainly different, but it may be no more difficult than in Paul's day.

We are called to engage with others. But how do we use pop culture language and imagery without sacrificing the integrity of the Gospel? Is it possible? If we are to present ourselves as holy people, should we refrain from mingling with the SimGospel's minions, such as TV, radio, and magazines? If we are all affected by this parasite of Christ's Gospel, should we avoid it? If it continually appeals to millions of followers, should we view it as competition?

Well, no. Caring for our neighbors requires us to be in the world. When God equips us with the Gospel, we can enter meaningful dialogue and expose what is counterfeit. As the truth is revealed, we may realize that we have been as affected by the SimGospel as others, but we will still serve as witnesses.

The apostle Paul wrote:

> I have voluntarily become a servant to any and all in order to reach a wide range of people. . . . I didn't take on their way of life. I kept my bearings in Christ—but I entered their world and tried to experience things from their point of view. I've become just about every sort of servant there is in my attempts to lead those I meet into a God-saved life. I did all this because of the Message. I didn't just want to talk about it; I wanted to be in on it! (1 Cor. 9:19–23)[2]

If we do not allow our Christian witness to speak clearly against the message of the SimGospel and the view of normal it creates, we will fail to serve our neighbors.

Human beings are products of a flawless original design, and the SimGospel promises daily that it can return us to that state. That is to say, Adam and Eve were given full identity and worth, as well as perfect harmony with God, each other, and the created order. When sin entered, they lost the reality of this flawless world, and to this day, our collective memory knows what it was like. Somehow, albeit with confusion, we remember Eden.

This is confirmed by our eagerness for restoration, and our willingness to settle for any proposed solutions, regardless of their viability. We are markedly influenced by the SimGospel's salvific message, and we are desperate to have what it simulates.

Again, if Christians fail to serve prophetically in such an environment of misdirected pursuits, we will fail at the fundamentals of taking Christ's Gospel into the world. It is Christ who uncovers the treason committed behind this fraudulent pulpit, and when we serve others—when we reach out to meet their needs—we witness to his ability and love.

Common ground

One of the most useful tools we have for reaching out is our familiarity with popular culture. Paul's comments in 1 Corinthians 9 (above) are a testimony to why this is important. While he names what enabled him to be a servant to everyone, he also reminds his readers of their responsibility to do the same. Familiarity, he argues, provides common ground for care to take place. He served his audience in a way that connected him with them, all the while keeping his bearings in Christ. But how do we become familiar in the twenty-first century?

I think this is a rather easy question to answer. Decades of watching TV and going to church got me there without effort. All that time, I was learning the language, imagery, and messages of both the TV world and Christianity. Familiarity was not my issue, and it may not be yours either. The problem, however, was this: I sat under two pulpits, claimed two memberships, and allowed minimal interaction between them.

When my faith matured enough to reveal that the content of television mimicked the Gospel's format, I suddenly awoke to my dualistic lifestyle. My familiarity was introduced to a new perspective, and it led me immediately to numerous insights regarding these two belief systems.

I will never forget when a former student experienced a similar wake-up call. Eve was a student leader on our wilderness team, and I had been privileged to watch her journey unfold. She had been raised in Sunday school and in private religious schools and had been taught all of the basic points of Christianity. She knew them and could recite them, but she lacked the ability to see beyond their surface value. In the summer following her sophomore year, however, she responded to God's call and committed her life to Christ.

Almost instantly the religious information that had accumulated throughout her childhood took on surprising depth. The terminology and concepts of the Gospel suddenly became significant and real, and they provided a new context for engagement with the world around her. Familiarity, when introduced to this wonderfully new perspective, enabled her to make sense of previous experiences and find meaning behind all she had spent her life consuming.

Perhaps I find this so exciting because Eve had been practicing mindless consumption in an attempt to fill significant voids. Although she was familiar with religious stuff, it was her encounter with Christ that gave it meaning. Her life really began when the SimGospel's emptiness was exposed, and Jesus's care welcomed. This gave her reason to believe that application of meaning-filled faith was paramount in every area of life. Because she had traveled so long with the SimGospel, she was very familiar with it. By applying her new faith, this familiarity provided common ground with others that was genuine, relevant, and effective as a witness to God's love.

Engagement: A nonnegotiable

I find familiarity with popular media in many of my social circles. There are always people who can join me in reciting commercial and movie lines, for example. We laugh over who said what, and what happened, and we often relate life events with popular media events: "That reminds me of [movie] when [actor] said. . . ." "Oh, yeah," someone replies, "I remember that!"

We are unbelievably familiar with this cultural topic, but the conversations could easily end with no more than the reminiscing of catchy lines if we are not careful. Whether it is the sophomore's religious background or a magazine lover's inside scoop on Hollywood stars, we must not stop short of interacting on a deeper level. Being able to discuss movies, then, should be seen as more than common ground for general conversation. The advertising that film and other media portray offers a string of sermonettes that persuade consumers to believe a certain way, and it is crucial that we address them thoughtfully.

This ideological persuasion is one of the SimGospel's more subtle tricks. Typically, we think of advertising as limited to thirty-second TV spots and magazine ads, but it is also important to see its presence in a three-hour blockbuster. Steve Garber even says that while the filmmaker "is arguing a point, sometimes very artfully, often very persuasively . . . it is 'impolite' to just sit there, passive and unresponsive."[3] He is saying that movies are hardly ever mindless, and I certainly agree, but I might add that it is also dangerous "to just sit there, passive and unresponsive." Unfortunately, entertainment and amusement have numbing effects on us, and we are discouraged from taking notes and paying close attention.

Look at the following definition and synonyms for *amuse:*

> amuse: to divert the attention of so as to deceive. . . . AMUSE, DIVERT, ENTERTAIN mean to pass or cause to pass the time pleasantly. AMUSE suggests that one's attention is engaged lightly or frivolously. DIVERT implies the distracting of the attention from worry or routine occupation esp. by something funny. ENTERTAIN suggests supplying amusement or diversion by specially prepared or contrived methods.[4]

Amuse is an interesting word, because *muse* means *think.* By adding the prefix *a,* which negates the word, we end up with a request to *turn off our brains.* The extent to which we consume the Gospel and the SimGospel is the extent to which we become familiar with them. When we consume much and engage little, with either of them, we become increasingly disengaged. Why do you think people say, "I didn't get anything out of it," when asked about a church experience? This too can become a form of amusement.

Let me summarize what I am saying:

1. My neighbor needs care.
2. I care by actively providing witness to God's love.
3. Witness requires engaging with others.
4. My most shared experience with others is through pop culture, where the primary voice is the SimGospel.
5. Engaging with others requires engaging with pop culture and understanding the influence of its various constituents, such as advertising.

If my faith is not applied to where it is most needed, and if it is given no voice to rival the SimGospel's preaching, then my witness will be rendered ineffective. I will neglect to care for my neighbor as she goes on consuming the stuff that will never meet her needs.

With Eve, my role as a campus minister was to intersect with her where she was at the time. And she would say that it was my witness of Christ's care (a testimony itself of the Holy Spirit's work) that propelled her forward.

So, how do we recover *muse*ment, and turn *on* our brains? In church, many people refuse to act like drones who assume that the pastor's words are straight from the Lord's mouth. They discuss with each other, critique the sermon, and write e-mails to him (or her) requesting explanations. Through this type of participation, they display wisdom.

The magic of the SimGospel, on the other hand, stands proudly behind its pulpit and delivers with eloquence and a slick tongue. Fixated on its dazzling performance, we are entertained enough to miss the heretical messages woven throughout it. (There are few e-mails sent to this pastor.)

This is where the Christian faith and its application come vitally into play. As we grasp the power of God's love, we will be freed to turn from the SimGospel's performance and to recognize its hypnotic abilities. We will be able to let go of its empty promises. We will also be able to let go of the pressures to conform. In loosing the debilitating grip of believing in SimGospel's idea of normal, we will be able to apply the depths of our faith in speaking informatively against its counterfeit messages. Familiarity will then breed context for meaning to emerge.

Here, our spiritual maturity becomes evident, and it highlights the presence of the Holy Spirit who intercedes for us. God's love becomes increasingly apparent, and our self-centeredness diminishes. His wisdom prevents us from missing the connection between familiarity and engagement, and we are provided with an attentive filter to discern the world around us. The insights we gain will permit us to see what our neighbors truly need (the same needs that, distorted, motivate them to adhere so tightly to the SimGospel), and with God's help we will offer genuine, relevant, and effective care. In this setting, neighbors will no longer be defined as the standard, or competitors, or nonentities, but rather as people whom we are to love on par with ourselves.

Gift giving

In this call to care for neighbors, our witness is to be shaped by Christ's model. When we volunteer to buy groceries and run errands for the housebound couple across the street, we offer loaves and fishes to the hungry. When we spend Tuesday and Thursday afternoons reading to city children and helping them with crafts, we model Jesus's love for children. When we invite a family to dinner whose kids show no respect for another's belongings, we may risk damage to our temporary treasures, but we offer a hospitality that heals.

Christine D. Pohl reminds us of the importance of gift giving:

> In hospitality, the stranger is welcomed into a safe, personal, and comfortable place, a place of respect and acceptance and friendship [even if they are not friendly or careful]. . . . Such welcome involves attentive listening and a mutual sharing of lives and life stories. It requires an openness of heart, a will-

ingness to make one's life visible to others, and a generosity of time and resources.[5]

Caring involves a giving away of self; an offering of what we have by way of talents and resources. As Pohl traveled the world, observing communities and researching the history of hospitality, she discovered certain principles to be true and necessary in order for people to thrive together:

> In the fourth century church leaders warned clergy . . . to welcome instead the poorest people to their tables. In doing so, they would have Christ as their guest. Wealthy female converts to Christianity become exemplary providers of Christian hospitality, using their family fortunes to offer food and shelter to the poor, sick, and pilgrims. They did not, however, use their wealth to exempt themselves from providing the care with their own hands.[6]

There are two points I want to make from this last quote. The first is that in closing our doors on people, even the most difficult people, we are closing our doors on Christ. If it is true that we are made in the image of God, then Christ can be seen in each of us. It isn't that *some* of us are made in God's image, or that some of us are made *more* in the image of God than others. Rather, we are all, equally, made in his image.

Henri Nouwen addresses this in his book *Reaching Out.* He says, "Reaching out to strangers was not just a reaching out to the long row of people who are so obviously needy . . . but also a reaching out to the promises they are bringing with them as gifts to their host."[7] Closing the doors on the Christ in others denies the opportunity for us to benefit from what they bring.

As we give hospitality and care, we free others to be themselves, which permits us to see more clearly how God has created them. As we discover their beautiful gifts, we see the characteristics of God (humor, intellect, gentleness, and the like); and the better we see God, the better we can care in ways that actually reflect the way God cares for us. This is the benefit of having Christ as our guest.

The second point I want to make is that care costs. Notice Pohl's comment that they "did not . . . use their wealth to exempt themselves from providing the care with their own hands." Working for a nonprofit organization, I know the immense value of receiving financial contributions to support my salary and ministry programs. Yet, according to Pohl, becoming an "exemplary provider" may require thinking beyond a bank check. For example, contributing financially to Habitat for Humanity is much different from contributing *physically* by volunteering to build one of their houses. Caring for our neighbors is an act of sacrifice involving a willingness to find out what their needs are, and then a diligence to respond appropriately.

I certainly know when my giving is done out of surplus: it's easy, it doesn't take up my time, it doesn't hurt my budget, and it usually involves some desire to be thanked, even if I refuse compensation when offered. On the other hand, when any of the above conditions are reversed, I feel the cost, and my desire is to avoid the situation. But this is also the moment when I most clearly sense Christ urging me to respond in faith. When I do, it is then that I see real needs met and the SimGospel crippled.

Work as an act of care

Care is usually linked with volunteer hours, financial contributions, hospitality, or sitting with a neighbor after his or her spouse has died. But quite often, and this is particularly sad within the Christian population, work (the 9 to 5, wage-earning kind) is not even considered for this list. If being a witness is the way we reveal God's love and character to the world, then it is essential that we have a kingdom vision at work.

Remember that care is a God-given task for all people at all times. If we compartmentalize where and when we care for neighbors, and exclude the world of work as a viable place to practice it, then this call becomes a part-time effort.

Now, most of us, especially if we are Christian, believe that we do care for our neighbor at work. We smile at co-workers, refill coffeepots, use Bible verses as screen savers, and so on. This is commendable behavior, but it seems incomplete. For that matter, there were Christians at Enron, so it makes me think that more witness is necessary.[8] Of course, we should always treat our co-workers with respect and dignity, and love them as God would love them, but a more comprehensive vision is regularly overlooked.

In many ways, our limited view of work is a by-product of consumerism. Recall the aspirations of students in Duke's school of business: "With few exceptions, they wanted three things—money, power, and things."[9] Our media-soaked culture flaunts these three as direct benefits of higher education. This deems college, and eventually work, as a means to an end.

The same mentality is propagated daily in countless forms of advertising and media, and the result is an inability to see work itself as a form of care. Physical therapists might see work primarily as care, but what about accountants . . . or marketing strategists?!

What if we could see work in a new way—as something for others instead of as a means to our own ends? What if we were able to see work from a biblical viewpoint? What if work were considered a gift to others, and a gift to God in the form of contributing to the building of his kingdom?

The word *calling* is defined as "a strong inner impulse toward a particular course of action esp. when accompanied by conviction of divine influence."[10] This definition sounds like a motivation for volunteering at a soup kitchen. However, the word *calling,* or *vocation,* is used most often when referring to career. At least, this is how Christians use it.

As I think about this definition and its job-affiliated context, a question comes to mind: if calling is associated with career, and it is a "divine influence" that convicts me toward a particular course of action, then how can a career be for my good alone? God never influences me towards self-absorption. I am a community member with the primary *call* to care for others. If this is so, then career is not for the purpose of collecting "money, power, and things" for myself. Rather, it is for some greater reason that I work.

Professor Brian Walsh offers a few grassroots questions to help us discover this greater reason. They are written for students of all ages and majors, but I say that they are wise counsels for anyone with a job also:

> We can begin to integrate our faith with our studies [our jobs] only if we are thoroughly grounded in the biblical vision of life. . . . What the Bible teaches on stewardship . . . will affect our thinking about economics and commerce. Do those implications suggest a different model for our relation to the Third World? Will a Christian political theorist develop a different view of politics considering what the Bible says about justice and the poor? Does healing in the Scripture . . . have an effect on our approach to health care or social work?[11]

God's calling will always have kingdom implications. To ignore these is to put us at the center and to neglect our care for others. Our task is to combine career with charity; to combine career with justice. In this way, work can serve as a vital means of worshipping God and serving, that is, *caring for*, others.

Throughout this section, it will be important to remember just how much influence the SimGospel has on this particular function of work. Besides its effects on identity and worth, and the complications it produces within relationships, the SimGospel wreaks havoc on our view of work. Obviously, wanting more stuff requires more labor hours and more ladder climbing. And advertising has never said, "OK, stop. You don't really need that eighth pair of shoes, the power windows, or the forty-inch flat-screen television." Until it does, though, we will continue to abuse work for the sake of obtaining these items and thousands more. From the SimGospel's standpoint, it is critical to obscure work's real purpose from us, because discovery would not only cripple the product industry, but also threaten to fill our emptiness.

To counterattack, calling should be approached with intent and conviction. Waking up one Tuesday morning and deciding that I should teach Spanish just because I liked my tenth-grade Spanish teacher was not exactly calling. That is not to say that God didn't make good use of my gifts during the years I taught. It is to say that my approach was too random to be considered intentionally other-oriented. Surely there are many aspects of the public school system in need of God's healing. Some of them are plain to see. But none of them is why I entered the field. With good memories of high school Spanish and a growing dislike for my engineering classes, I decided on a career. Neighbors excluded.

Frederick Buechner states,

> The kind of work God usually calls you to do is the kind of work (a) that you need most to do and (b) that the world most needs to have done. If you really get a kick out of your work, you've presumably met requirement (a), but if your work is writing TV deodorant commercials, the chances are you've missed requirement (b). On the other hand, if your work is being a doctor in a leper colony, you have probably met requirement (b), but if most of the time you are bored and depressed by it, the chances are you have not only by-passed (a) but probably aren't helping your patients much either. . . . The place God calls you to is the place where your deep gladness and the world's deep hunger meet.[12]

Work is a meaningful way to worship God, to bless others, and to use our gifts.

At the heart of work is service. Furthering cures for diseases, picking up recycling bins at 2 a.m., removing stress by covering the details for a boss, raising children, stewarding an institution's money, guiding people into the Grand Canyon to see the wonders of creation, making Band-Aids that not only improve healing but also leave body hair in place, farming land to provide balanced diets, hanging phone lines to promote communication, and studying physics in order to construct safe bridges are all acts of service. Of course, there are jobs that fail to benefit humanity, such as managing an "adult" bookstore or working as marketing director for a casino.

In addition to these few exceptions, higher education appears to be seriously lacking in its formation of care-oriented graduates. What if students had to sign a responsibility clause upon entering college? Perhaps it would read:

> I, the undersigned, hereby recognize that the chief end of academic study is threefold, and ranks in the following order:
>
> 1. To develop the skills necessary to more effectively welcome the kingdom of God, for the sake of the glory of God, by specializing in a chosen field of study.
> 2. To love my neighbor as myself through the act of vocational service.
> 3. To thoroughly enjoy the gifts imparted to me as a reflection of the Creator's magnificent imagination.
>
> I claim that these are true and worthy of my utmost attention throughout and beyond the ensuing college years.
>
> Signed _____

Is it possible to recover this perspective, considering the radical threat it would pose to consumer mentality? What would it do to the SimGospel's presence if swarms of graduates entered their particular fields with the intent of caring for their neighbors and blessing God? This would be radical indeed!

A look at Genesis reveals that God modeled this kind of caring work from the beginning. He worked to bring order to the universe, to make something that would reflect his creativity, and to glorify himself. He made people, bearers of his image, and put them "in the Garden of Eden to work it and take care of it" (Gen. 2:15). Then God rested on the seventh day because of "all the work of creating that he had done" (Gen. 2:3).

Work is a noble task we are called to do, and we are called to it for the purpose of serving the Creator and the created order. When we work with this intent, we worship God. When we work we reflect the image of our God who values work. How beautiful this attribute of the Creator, instilled in the people of his creation!

Calling requires us to set aside our own agendas so that we can discern God's purpose for us. Second, it requires that we ask how he wants that purpose to be carried out. When I am obedient to God's response, the SimGospel is stripped of its authority, and others are provided with care. Note the following examples of this from scripture.

Moses led the Israelites out of captivity; Jeremiah spoke hard words of truth to beckon the people back to holiness; Daniel studied foreign affairs and remained faithful to God in the midst of living in a godless culture; Nehemiah became a foreman and built a wall to restore dignity; the Pharisee Gamaliel counseled with sound wisdom to deal with citizens; and Lydia made clothing and provided housing for her honored guests.

For Christians, our work is shaped by Jesus's vision of the kingdom of God. When he prayed to the Father, he asked, "[May] your Kingdom come. May your will be done on earth as it is in heaven" (Luke 11:2). Jesus had a clear vision of restoration, and he knew how far we were from it. He grasped how fractured our understanding of relationships, work, and rest had become. Therefore, he knew the significance of teaching this prayer to his disciples. By giving them these words, he was also telling me how to pray 2,000 years later. And as I pray them, I have to ask what attributes of God's will in heaven need to be replicated on earth in order to move toward restoration. Otherwise, I'm just spitting out rote prayer without concern of God's will being done now.

Jesus knew that care had to be at the heart of his followers' lives. "Love each other as I have loved you," he commanded them (John 15:12). Setting "as I have loved you" as the benchmark revealed that he not only brought care to us, but brought care *as it is in heaven.* In coming as God in human flesh, he taught us how to treat our neighbors, but he also gave us a glimpse of the kingdom as it should be on earth.

If this isn't what he came to do, then what's the point of healing a maimed hand if the kingdom is not here? Why don't we just take a spiritual Gospel into the world and leave physical sickness and social injustices alone? Why shouldn't we all be pastors and youth leaders and church secretaries and avoid *secular* careers? What heavenly good could it possibly do to become Christian accountants, or Christian lawyers, or Christian carpenters if we are only going to share the *spiritual* Gospel with others? In other words, if Christian faith has no relevance to the accounting world, then why don't we just do accounting under the SimGospel's model?

This inadequate approach amounts to caring for others by telling them about Jesus, but it does nothing to address the fractures in the systems where they work.

Approaches to building the kingdom of God

Because of advertising's culture-saturating presence, and because of the SimGospel's power to infuse advertising with characteristics like me-focus and overconsumption, and because work can provide the primary means to achieve these selfish goals, it is imperative that we reclaim work for the sake of the Gospel. I'd like to suggest four approaches Christians most often take toward the relationship between faith and work. For those who work outside of the church (people other than pastors, youth leaders, etc.), it is easy to set aside the word *ministry* and go about work in whatever way *secular* jobs are predefined. And the result? Work is allowed to take on an inferior role as a SimGospel constituent.

The first approach to being a Christian employee (whose calling is to care for others) is to simply remain oblivious— thoughtless—about what is entailed in the job. You might say, "I leave my Christianity at church and home because it's private. I just want to be a good employee."

Another similar approach is to recognize the inconsistencies in the company and decide to secretly not support what it does. You might say, "I know I should probably say something because it isn't right how they're treating the folks down in shipping, but I need to pay bills and hold on to my benefits. I'll just do my job and get out of here at the end of the day."

A third is to take just a portion of faith to work. You might say, "I don't agree with some of the company's values, but who am I to change them? All I know is that I work with a lot of non-Christians who couldn't care less about God. So I take my Bible and read it in the lunchroom. I also have a scripture verse on my screen saver and a cross hanging in my cubicle. I really believe that I am a good and brave witness for the Lord in my job. No 'Sunday only Christianity' for me!"

This third one begins to resemble faithfulness, but like the others, it is still insufficient. A fourth and more biblically consistent approach considers work as an act of worship. It sees integration between faith and how the job is carried out. Here, you might say, "Not only is it important for me to pray on Tuesday mornings with Matt from human resources, but it's imperative that I speak up about the new business proposal because it conflicts with the service component of the company's mission." This approach cares for others, takes responsibility for how the company is managed, and honors the Lord. But the risk of being criticized or even fired is greater.

You *could* remain silent.

You *could* leave your convictions at home.

You *could* convey full support of the company by your silence on shady issues, even while sharing your personal faith with coworkers.

However, choosing the fourth option is a more thoughtful, caring move that denounces SimGospel traits. Here you might begin by peering behind nicely wrapped packages on your employer's shelves to see who packaged them, and then researching where and for how little and under what conditions the work was done. Or you might consider how your store's products are marketed and whether those techniques promote individualism, greed, and a lust for more frivolity. Whatever the case, this approach calls managers, cart boys, legal aides, and CEOs alike on ethical "bendings." Ultimately, the fourth option comes from realizing that a paycheck is worth more when your vision of the kingdom acts as a litmus test for how to work.

Paraphrasing James 2:17, "Faith at work, without deeds that affect *dis*integrated corporate systems, is dead."

Work is an expression of care for the creation and care for our neighbors. And when we do it with integrity, we can convert it from its common use as a supply line for selfish consumption into a gift. But in order to do this, there must be insight as to what is whole or complete or without any further need of care. When my daughter hands me her toy fire truck whose ladder has separated, I know what to do because I know how a toy fire truck should be. Brokenness can only be known in reference to wholeness. Otherwise, I have no reference point for what care is or how far it should be applied.

When there is no vision, work becomes filler between paydays, and where there is no vision, the SimGospel will produce its own if it thinks it can perpetuate materialistic goal setting and overconsumption. I'm not referring to vision such as "I want to grow this company until it becomes international." I mean the kind that captures a glimpse of perfection—a glimpse of the way life was intended to be. If I can creatively imagine what life would look like without surrogate gods and vain pursuits, how might work appear? Work certainly existed before the fall. It was not a curse given to Adam and Eve. The hardness of work was part of the curse, but even in the midst of it being difficult, I can still imagine how it might have been.

Imagine refuse companies in the Garden of Eden before sin ever tarnished the good creation. Imagine homemaking, road building, secretarial duties, accounting, and the writing of dictionaries. These would all have had to be done eventually, so what would they have looked like?

This glimpse compels us to see our work not only as care for others, but also as a gift to God. Using our talents and wisdom to better the world is an act of worship, and no field is excluded (except for those few that work against the kingdom). So, God is worshipped when I pick up the neighbor's dog-strewn trash. But God is also worshipped when I am a corporate accountant who considers the subsidiary companies and working-class people affected by my stewardship.

A gift to God, our Host

As the rain and the snow come down from heaven, and do not return to it without watering the earth and making it bud and flourish, so that it yields seed for the sower and bread for the eater, so is my word that goes out from my mouth: It will not return to me empty, but will accomplish what I desire and achieve the purpose for which I sent it. (Isa. 55:10–11)

God delights in gift giving. By serving others, we bless him, and this is perhaps the greatest reason to care for others. Jesus said that by caring for the least in society (the most difficult ones to care for), we care for him. Regarding work, God has marked each of us with a special purpose—some kind of gift that makes your work uniquely different from my work. To use these in service to others is to respond to God in an honoring way. The saying goes, "Our talents are God's gift to us. What we do with them is our gift to God." The blessing and curse is that we can use his gifts as we so choose. As a result, we occasionally hide them, we frequently abuse them, and we rarely give them back. Daniel gave them back.

In a foreign land under a godless king, the Jewish captive Daniel honored the Lord with his gifts. "To [Daniel] God gave knowledge and understanding of all kinds of literature and learning. And Daniel could understand visions and dreams of all kinds" (Dan. 1:17). This was the special way God had marked him—the way in which Daniel could best serve others. And Daniel did worship the Lord by serving others, even though his "neighbors" were also his captors. He spent sixty years bearing witness to God amidst the Babylonian people, and his prayer reveals the intentions of his heart: "Praise be to the name of God for ever and ever. . . . I thank and praise *you*, O God. . . . *You* have given me wisdom and power, *you* have made known to me what we asked of you, *you* have made known to us the dream of the King . . ." (Dan. 2:20, 23, italics mine).

Daniel gave to the Giver by giving what he had to others, and I suppose that God took great delight in this.

The Host's gift to us

We too take delight in gift giving. Ironically, while work benefits others as it worships God, its outcome results in personal fulfillment. Daniel knew that God was pleased by his faithfulness, and he continued to serve. It pleased *him* to know that he could bring pleasure to God. John Piper claims that "God is most glorified in me when I am most satisfied in him."[13] He suggests that this is a reflexive relationship, eventually resulting in what he calls "Christian Hedonism."

Christian Hedonism is simply this: finding deep pleasure in knowing that the "climax of [God's] happiness is the delight he takes in the echoes of his excellence in the praises of the saints."[14] When I know that he delights in the praises of his saints (you and me), and that the praises of his saints are found in the reflecting of his image (seen in our care for others and use of our gifts), then I delight in knowing that my Christian witness has the effect of pleasing God.

I have experienced this on several backpacking trips with students. Each time, a special moment confirmed that I was in just the right place at just the right time. My friend refers to it this way: "Every molecule of my being was oriented towards God." In these moments, I know that what I offered to the group through teaching, listening, allowing them to fail, or rejoicing in their growth, was just the right thing at the right time. In these moments, I experienced deep fulfillment in my work because my unique gifts were shaping how I did my job. Often times, unfortunately, it is my job that dictates the gifts, but I prefer the other way.

When my gifts sit at the center of my work, every day reveals confirmations of the special ways God has designed me. Out of this deep sense of fulfillment, I find it easier to worship—at least, it seems to flow more naturally. It is, in some ways, how God intended it: his design "yields seed for the sower and bread for the eater" for his own glory. And by serving as the hands and feet through which this happens, I experience deep satisfaction.

Our gift to neighbors

Our neighbors delight in our gift giving. This has been the topic of the chapter, and I want to conclude with it.

By faithful response to Christ's presence in me, others are cared for. When we give, we serve as a witness to who God is, and to how he loves his children. And it makes no difference whether we give by volunteering on Saturdays or punching in daily at 8:00 a.m. Through this testimony, others can experience the same process for themselves:

> God sends seed and bread to the body of Christ. You respond by passing these on as a faithful steward. I (your neighbor), receive adequate provision from your care. God is blessed.
>
> God sends more seed and bread. I respond by passing these on. My neighbor now receives care from me. God is blessed.
>
> God sends more. My neighbor passes them on. Her neighbor is now cared for . . .

It can be a glorious chain reaction. Unfortunately, the cycle rarely happens in this ideal way. Gift giving is difficult. We are naturally prone to self-centeredness, and the SimGospel takes full advantage of our weakness. We are constantly reminded that neighbors are people to climb over for the sake of comfort and status. Furthermore, everywhere we turn, advertising retells the story that we aren't enough; we don't have enough; we're not successful enough. And our response often reflects a belief that these statements are true.

Gift giving and a God-centered work ethic are antidotes. Even in the midst of self-centeredness and highlighted inadequacies, the question, "What does my neighbor need?" still exists. And each of us is still responsible for answering it. Counteracting the SimGospel by honoring the Lord requires active observation and listening to the lives of our neighbors.

Most often, what we see and hear calls for sacrifice. I certainly can't expect to live well by ignoring the call to sacrifice, so I try to respond, and this leads to enough "success" that I keep on trying.

Neglect is easy to commit and difficult to detect, especially when I assume center stage and do a half-good job at it.

7

A Neglected Member

How do I neglect my neighbor?

In chapter 5, I presented three ways the SimGospel influences us to answer the question, "Who is my neighbor?" They were:

1. *the standard,* seen as the ideal, but unrealistic goal to achieve;
2. *competition,* seen as keeping up with the Joneses; and,
3. *the nonentity,* reducing the neighbor (especially women) to subhuman status.

In chapter 6, I asked the question "What does my neighbor need?" and I answered it by exploring the gift of care through volunteerism and work. In summary, neighbors need care, and the SimGospel treats neighbors in a way that doesn't elicit care.

So, we know what the SimGospel does, but this chapter will underscore the importance of taking responsibility for our actions. We can't say, "The SimGospel made me do it!" That is a cop-out.

Acts of gratuity are hard to come by. Certainly, it is good to feel pleasure in giving, as in the way we find deep satisfaction when God is pleased, but when our motive is based on getting a return, integrity is diminished.

A campus I worked at has a new student center, and every room has a donor plaque hanging on the wall. The donors don't own these spaces, but their names are forever engraved so that all who pass by will know of their generosity. Perhaps this practice inspires others to give. But when I hear of donors complaining about their plaques being hung in nondescript corners of the building—"I gave a lot of money. I should be displayed more prominently!"—I have to question how genuine their motive in giving was in the first place.

We need recognition and we need to know that we are significant. Unfortunately, we often reach for these needs in self-glorifying ways and trample others in order to advance our standing. It is good to care for ourselves, but when neighbors suffer at the expense of our overindulgence, what happens to them?

First John 3:17 states, "If anyone has material possessions and sees his brother in need but has no pity on him, how can the love of God be in him?" The same verse in The Message reads, "If you see some brother or sister in need and have the means to do something about it but turn a cold shoulder and do nothing, what happens to God's love? It disappears. And you made it disappear."[1]

In a culture saturated with stuff, God's wisdom is essential in determining our true needs. If we could discern and be as shrewd as snakes; if we could cap our satisfaction levels; if we could govern our want-o-meters and tune out those voices that for so long have spoken directly to us in very personal terms, we might counter the effects of the SimGospel and its helpers. Unfortunately, we continue to strive for what the SimGospel's idea of normal, which requires constant attention to self. Until we step away from the SimGospel, there will be little room for neighbors.

Even when we do *recognize* how we neglect them, *responding* actively is an entirely different thing.

Every Thanksgiving, my family gathers for the typical holiday festivities. After dinner and some televised football, the twenty or so of us, including children, reconvene at the table to share tales of God's provision in the last year. It is a significant time, and it really pulls the family together. Couples tell of marriage hardships; individuals share the grief associated with loss or the diagnosis of illness; children humble the adult intellect with their simple faith; and we rejoice over new births, support received from each other, and financial stability.

A few years ago I noticed several who specifically mentioned how blessed we are as Americans. Let us remember developing countries, they said. Let us not take for granted the food, clothing, and shelter we have.

It was good to hear, especially as we had spent the day indulging in that same American wealth. Yet, perhaps due to my cynicism, or more likely, my personal guilt, I wondered how many of those words had substance. I mean, Thanksgiving is twofold. First, it is naming the gifts we have received. But second, it is doing something with them. That is to say, it has a second part.

While it is necessary and right to praise God for our blessings, it would be tragic to stop where someone like Zacchaeus picked up. Zacchaeus's encounter with Jesus led to naming what he had as a wealthy tax collector, but then it resulted in action: "Look, Lord! Here and now I give half of my possessions to the poor, and if I have cheated anybody out of anything, I will pay back four times the amount" (Luke 19:8). Interestingly, Jesus called this "salvation."

In the very same chapter of Luke's Gospel, we read of the king who gave financial responsibilities to his servants. Two of them reported high earnings from wise investments. But the third servant had done nothing with his portion. When the king learned of this, he took away what little the servant had. As Americans, we have a larger portion of wealth than most of the world's population. Jesus's exhortations to be responsible with it are just as applicable today as they were on the streets of Jericho.

Thanks is only half of it; *giving* is the other half.

It is good to be thankful, and it is Christian to give to others. But often, as Steve Garber states, our telos does not line up with our praxis. In other words, what we believe about the world and its purpose often fails to line up with how we live in the world. Garber's book *The Fabric of Faithfulness* looks at this disintegration as it pertains to college students. He believes that students who display integration between their telos and praxis will be those who make prophetic and healing contributions both to their professions and to the world at large.[2] They will be citizens whose *thanks* lines up with their *giving*.

When we enter careers primarily to earn money and establish security and status for ourselves, observers should not be surprised when we thank God but exclude sacrificial giving. I can't judge the hearts of my family members, nor can I claim exemption from guilt (certainly I am guilty!), but it frightens me to see how long we all go without visibly demonstrating radical kingdom thanks and giving. "[F]aith by itself, if it is not accompanied by action, is dead" (James 2:17). "Me first" as a philosophy cannot produce care for others in a substantial way.

The SimGospel profits from our self-centeredness and capitalizes on displacing our neighbors. We have no problem developing a "me first" attitude on our own, but advertising reinforces this disposition. Furthermore, it attempts (perhaps inadvertently) to erase possibilities for living well in community. By confirming that we deserve every product on the market at the expense of others, the SimGospel encourages neglect. With this inundation of reinforcement, it is terribly difficult to escape the Gospel's nemesis.

Mine!

Neglect is the cause of many types of harm, and much of the perpetration is due to the way we approach ownership. My house, my money, my new car, my natural resources, my property, my country, my woman, my God . . . *my* and *mine* are ownership words, assimilated at a very early age into the vocabulary and behavior of children. And what is mine must be protected, or else it will no longer be mine. This becomes the case especially when the value we place on temporary items exceeds healthy levels.

St. Thomas Aquinas states that people "ought to possess external things, not as [their] own, but as common, so that, to wit, [they are] ready to communicate them to others in their need."[3] Ownership is good, but only under the condition that it must be held with regard for the neighbor who is in need. "The earth is the LORD's, and everything in it, the world, and all who live in it; for he founded it upon the seas and established it upon the waters" (Ps. 24:1–2).

Distracted by surplus

Surplus is an odd word, especially since most of the world endures inadequate conditions. But our stores are jammed with toys and clothing and cars and food. As far as we know, it's like that everywhere. I walked into a neighborhood market that had very few items on its shelves. I asked the clerk if they were closing down, and she said, "No. Why?" Living in a "stocked" environment has serious effects on our awareness of

123

others. The ways in which we pursue material goods, perceive available natural resources, and relate to the larger community are clear indicators that our awareness is low.

"It's not more than you need. Just more than you're used to," says a GM truck ad. Give it time. We'll get used to it.

Material goods have a way of requiring great amounts of attention and they easily distract us from others. We feel the need to protect what we've acquired, to polish what is expensive, and to store what may lose value if left out in the weather. To paraphrase King Solomon: "The abundance of the rich permits no sleep" (Eccles. 5:12b).

I don't believe that Jesus commands us to renounce all possessions. Yet, when possessions act as an immediate substitute for what can come only through faith and patience, our experience of God's immanence is blocked, and we lose our sense of place in the created order. The pursuit of self-serving riches is incompatible with God's will, and it steals time that would be better invested in others. As a result, our indulgence leads to neglect.

More for me . . . less for you

Self-centeredness and excessive consumption deter us from caring for others. One indicator is found in the way we perceive available natural resources. The earth regenerates itself in many ways, but when we consume resources faster than they can be replaced, an obvious problem arises.

Imagine that what I consume and waste throughout my lifetime is measured in acres. I consume through bathing, heating my house, washing clothes, turning on lamps, and buying stuff. I produce waste by changing car oil, tossing food wrappers and diapers, disposing of old tires, and using more than what I need (e.g., running a dishwasher that is half full). All of us consume and produce waste in order to survive. That is how God created us, and he made the earth renewable to sustain this design.

124

This acre measurement is known as my "ecological footprint."[4] It is the mark I leave on the earth. Of course, there is a finite number of acres available, and if they were divided among all people, I would receive a certain finite portion. There are enough sustainable resources in the world if they are used properly, but problems occur when the balance is tilted and we use more acres than we ought:

In the United States, the average ecological footprint is 31 acres per person. But what our planet has available for us to use—in sheer life-supporting land mass—is 5 acres per person. . . . If everyone around the globe consumed resources and produced waste at our rate—and if our planetary population did not grow at all—we would need six Earths to meet everyone's demands.[5]

I understand it like this: Julie and I often have students over for pizza. If there are five of us, I don't order one large pie. I get at least two and maybe something more, because I always want enough for everyone to have their fill. Unfortunately, my overestimation usually leads to gluttony for at least half of us. "Having their fill" for Americans most commonly means super-sized portions.

"From the late 1970s to the mid-1990s, food portions in America grew by around 60 percent, and diets contained more unhealthy, salty foods. . . . Over two decades . . . the average portion size of salty snacks grew by 60 percent; soft drink sizes expanded 50 percent; hamburger portions grew by 23 percent, and French fry portions grew by 16 percent."[6] These are indicators that we take more than our share.

My pizza order does not require anyone to sacrifice for the sake of the others. I ask Bill, "How many pieces can you eat?" I want to know his max, and the max is what I give him. If I don't buy enough, then I feel awkward when the food is gone too soon. Why? Because rationing isn't easy. You know how it feels when there isn't enough. The one remaining piece lies there with no comfortable place to go. It isn't extra, so people want it. There isn't enough to go around again, so the givers surrender and the takers eat what remains.

With pizza, I rarely ask folks to take the fewest number of slices possible. Therefore, Bill doesn't have to make sure there is enough for everyone. He can eat until he is full—no hesitations, no looking around.

The SimGospel never highlights what acreage is available to us. In fact, it hides limits and discards stewardship as a way of life. When we lose awareness in this area, we no longer have reason to even consider an ecological footprint. Instead, we hear, "Consume, consume, consume," and we obey without calculating how much is available or how much we are shortchanging our neighbors. Our resources will sustain us within reason, but they cannot endure reckless disregard. It is a simple equation: if we take too much, others will have to settle for less.

But is all this attributed to greed? Indirectly, yes, but when we have no physical or personal connection with people in Brazil or Indonesia, we don't always realize that our excessive consumption is stealing from them. Remember, I thought the neighborhood market was going out of business because the shelves were half empty. We live in a stocked environment and that makes a significant impression on us.

The earth's table is too big to see across. It is difficult and sometimes impossible to tell what others either have or don't have on their plates. So, we live as if it were an all-you-can-eat pizza night. We see the surplus, so we use it, or eat it, or buy it.

Imagine treating the acres of our ecological footprint like points in a Weight Watchers diet. There is a lot of freedom in how we use the points, but certain resources cost more than others do. We have the right to go over in points, but it defeats the purpose of the diet, which is to add health to us and the world. On the actual Weight Watchers diet, it hurts only you if you go over. On the world scale, however, every point over—every acre over—hurts *somebody else*. From an ethical standpoint, we might as well steal the lawn mower from our next-door neighbor's garage. Either way it is thievery.

We let the water run while brushing our teeth and take twenty-minute showers; we drive one mile to the store when we could ride a bike or walk, and we use sixty-watt bulbs where we could use forties; we pass out Styrofoam plates when we could eat right out of the box; we use fresh sheets of paper instead of used when printing nonessential documents, and we get a new disposable cup every day for lunch at work. Regarding food, "Americans toss the equivalent of more than 21 million grocery bags full of perfectly good food into landfills every year."[7]

Using our acres wisely requires discipline, awareness, and measuring. For most of us, this is a foreign concept. Because we have difficulty experiencing others' hunger, we have very little capacity or context for care. The SimGospel's powerful message keeps our awareness just too low.

Cold enough for you?

Throughout my camping years, I've acquired all of the necessary clothing and accessories to be comfortable in the woods. If it's wet, I can stay dry. If it's cold, I can stay warm.

Two years ago, I was hiking in George Washington National Forest in Virginia with a group of 10–15 students. My two student leaders and I had headlamps (like miner's lamps that rest on your forehead), while the rest of the first-time campers did not.

On the first night, we arrived late to our designated campsite, which resulted in setting up camp in complete darkness. No problem, I thought as I donned my headlamp. But one student caught my attention as she struggled to find warm layers, a water bottle, bandanas, and eating utensils. Of course, this always happens with new hikers, especially disorganized ones, but what I noticed specifically was the difficulty she had with her flashlight. It was too big to hold with her teeth, too heavy to prop between her shoulder and head, and too cumbersome for reaching into a tall, narrow backpack.

Realizing that I had something she could probably use, I gave her my headlamp. With gratitude, she put it on and quickly found the missing items. Over the next few days, I watched how each new person experienced discomfort where I had none. Experience and accurate purchases had created a level of comfort for me that they didn't know existed. When they were cold or wet or uncomfortable, I was not.

For the first time I became aware that my comfort had hidden their discomfort from me. I reminisced about the times when folks must have been freezing in coats that weren't waterproof. And I could think of many who must have endured terrible discomfort while hiking in poor-fitting boots.

Once comfort becomes so comfortable, it is easy to forget that someone else might need what I do not. There is a strong correlation between focus on personal comfort and neglect for others' comfort, just as material wealth and a satisfied belly can distance me from the poor and hungry. It's not always intentional—it just seems to happen.

I will share one more example of how awareness affects our care for others.

Oh, there's someone else in line?

My family and I attended one of our church's monthly beach services. It always begins with a potluck picnic dinner and Tim cooking hot dogs. On this particular occasion, Tim was unable to come, and no arrangements had been made for the entrée. Furthermore, an unusually small crowd meant fewer selections of side dishes.

First, because there were fewer options, I knew I would have to eat foods that I normally wouldn't (sacrifice is rarely necessary when there is surplus). Second, I was toward the front of the line and came to a salad bowl that was *already* nearly finished. I glanced back at the hungry parishioners behind me to get a general census before estimating how much, if any, I could reasonably take. When I reached the dessert section, I had to refrain from gorging on some delicious brownies, because they too were almost gone. It occurred to me that on every other occasion, there was so much surplus that not only could I avoid personally unpleasant foods, but I could also eat more than my fill without even a slight consideration for others.

Now, it should be said that I am a tall, thin man who enjoys eating. But I can skip a meal when necessary, so what I faced here was in no way catastrophic. There was still enough food for everyone, and I was full when finished, but the fact that I glanced back to know how much I should save for others caught my usually self-centered attention. In that brief moment, I recognized a trademark of the SimGospel: having too much promotes apathy.

Combining the problem of surplus with the size of the earth's table, I can only see to consume what lies in front of me, which usually amounts to more than enough. When people sit too far away, it is difficult to tell if they have enough, or even if they have any at all. Consequently, it costs nothing to think about them. I may gluttonously indulge, or simply just consume until I'm satisfied. Either way, my distant neighbors and their needs are out of sight and out of mind, and the SimGospel displays its effectiveness once again.

In the second half of this chapter, you will see that much of the content is interchangeable with the first half. For instance, individuals make ecological footprints, but they are also corporately made by nations. Wealthy countries such as America make enormous footprints.

For the second half, I suggest thinking about the material on a corporate level. That is to say, what kind of damage is committed when you and I, and my neighbor and your neighbor, and my town and your town, and so on, all act carelessly at the same time? What influence does the SimGospel have on our corporate body called America with regard to its treatment of the rest of the world?

How do we collectively neglect our neighbors?

> You have hoarded wealth in the last days. Look! The wages you failed to pay the workmen who mowed your fields are crying out against you. The cries of the harvesters have reached the ears of the Lord Almighty. You have lived on earth in luxury and self-indulgence. You have fattened yourselves as in a day of feasting. (James 5:2–5)

> "Woe to him who piles up stolen goods and makes himself wealthy by extortion! How long must this go on?" (Hab. 2:6–8)

Do not collect $200

A student told me that she didn't play Monopoly as a kid because she didn't like what it did to her siblings. The game is based on hoarding and self-indulgence, and it does seem to bring out the worst in people. If you have ever played it with friends or family, you might know this. At least one of you, if not all, will take great pleasure in rising to power. Others will swoop low emotionally once they've landed on enough properties to be drained financially. Factions and loyalties can occur; competitive players easily intensify, and when the game is over it can feel like forgiveness is needed. I'm not saying that it isn't fun to play. It's just that power and greed, whether in a board game or in real life, do the opposite of caring.

I can recall times when friends turned into the likeness of Gollum, a creature whose greed consumed him at the expense of all else and all others.[8] It's as if they suddenly turned evil, and it made me want to end the game.

There is nothing mysterious about Monopoly and its Chance cards, Free Parking, Go to Jail, and Boardwalk. But *monopoly* is control by an individual or a select few. In the game, this means property. When we control little, we are at the mercy of dominant property owners. When big money is at stake, we are at the mercy of the dice. When we hit rock bottom, we are at the mercy of players who may or may not lend dollars to hold us over (that's a rule I sometimes add). Without control, the game can be frustrating, because we are failing at the very point of it. And when we are failing, it means that someone else is succeeding. Furthermore, the successful are probably enjoying it so much that their joy becomes envied and their money is coveted: "If only I had one or two of his dark orange $500 bills, I could get out of this mess." But, it's only a game, right?

Most of us can afford to buy Monopoly for somewhere around $25, but many real-life players can afford to bargain for oil fields and international clothing-manufacturing companies. I don't have the cash to purchase a multinational corporation, but some do. This is where the game comes to life. Greed and power in my living room have real-world counterparts of international proportions, and they threaten the global landscape.

Naomi Klein documents some of these real-world "monopolizers" in *No Logo*. She argues that in business, we often take advantage of the poor to pocket a few more dollars. But when the poor are hidden by the glamour of accumulating products made by their sweat, we become oblivious.

Increasingly, brand-name multinationals—Levi's, Nike, Champion, Wal-Mart, Reebok, the Gap, IBM and General Motors—insist that they are just like any one of us: bargain hunters in search of the best deal in the global mall. They are very picky customers, with . . . the need for rock-bottom prices. But what they are not interested in is the burdensome logistics of how those prices fall so low; building factories, buying machinery and budgeting for labor have all been lobbed squarely into somebody else's court . . . somebody has to get down and dirty and make the products the global brands will hang their meaning on.[9]

A friend of mine recently co-led a group of college students to Honduras for a service trip. Many of the people they served work in nearby *maquiladoras,* or sweatshops, owned by brand-name multinationals like those listed above. Their hourly wage is thirty-three lempira, and they work more than sixty hours a week. That's $1.90 an hour in U.S. dollars, or less than $6,000 a year, with no benefits.[10] Suddenly, minimum wage in the U.S. doesn't sound too bad.

Why is this the case? "At the end of this [subcontracting] chain is the worker . . . with a paycheck that has been trimmed at every turn. 'When the multinationals squeeze the subcontractors, the subcontractors squeeze the workers . . .'"[11]

In *Rich Christians in an Age of Hunger,* Ron Sider adds excellent insight on the role that these multinational corporations often play:

> MNCs are on the cutting edge of industrialized nations' contact with the people of developing nations. MNCs thus communicate to a poverty-stricken world what life is like in affluent nations. But . . . they also encourage them, through lavish advertising campaigns, to try and live the same way.
>
> The result is that . . . many poor people are enticed into spending a disproportionate share of their incomes on goods of little value. . . . Even more outrageous are the aggressive advertising campaigns of U.S. tobacco companies in poor nations."[12]

The other monopoly effect that caught my friend's attention was observed in the participating students. Many of them confessed that they came for vacation, and a few because it would look good on their résumés! Further, these arrogant students marveled at the help they offered to the Hondurans without realizing how much they needed the Hondurans to teach them.

Our mind-set toward consumption and numbness in a culture of plenty has enormous effects on our collective treatment of others. It is one thing to play a board game, and quite another when real people with real needs are at stake.

Overconsumption

The SimGospel never tells us to curb our consumption. It never tells us to shop in moderation. We don't see commercials (unless they are for churches or charity organizations, but that isn't our focus here) for the local grocery chain that say, "The next time you come to Great Foods grocery store, consider buying 25 percent fewer items for the same amount of meals and people."

We are not advised to cut back on our gluttony, even though it is what promotes the squeezing cycle that oppresses *maquiladora* workers. The problem begins with my receiving and adopting the message not to slow down. It continues when I support uncaring MNCs (through employment, clothing purchases, etc.). By doing this, I join a corporation of people who also do not want to slow down. The corporation and I are bargain hunters in search of the best deal. It's just that one of us shops locally, while the other shops abroad. One of us leaves small tracks; the other, large swaths of impact. It is easy to forget, however, that a bunch of me makes the large swaths.

We live in, and create, a culture of overconsumption, and we seldom regard the victims along the way. We want to be satisfied, and we want nothing to stand in our way.

Andy is a graduate student in the Environmental Studies program at Miami University of Ohio. While taking a class on environmental resources, he called me one afternoon in frustration. It had to do with the approach his class and professors were taking:

> We look at natural resources, how they're used, and how much is left of them, and we consider what new resources we can

use when the current ones either subside to dangerously low levels or else become exhausted. But we're missing a major factor for why our resources are in danger in the first place: we consume too much! What if we were to focus on ways to cut back on resources we're currently using instead of just lining up new ones to be used at the same careless and "unstewardly" rate?

His question would eventually lead him to research *sustainable development.* This is a buzzword in the environmental field. It considers the balance between growth and stewardship and provides a model whereby a poor country can sustain itself economically and environmentally. It's sort of like teaching a person how to fish instead of just giving him a fish. It is not like pure capitalism that rampantly seeks profit, yet it requires profit in order to create sustainability.

When we consume without prudence, we mistreat the resources God has put in our care. And we neglect our neighbors who need those resources for adequate provision. If *all* developing countries were given our North American model, which consumes too many resources, creates too much pollution, and defies sustainability, imagine the horrendous threat we would become collectively.

Andy is aware that God has called him to care for others and for the creation. It is very exciting to know that he will be working in this field to address our insatiable lust for more.

Hey, I was here first!

In September of 1893, the U.S. government forced the Cherokee Strip to be sold. In order to give interested citizens equal access to this Indian territory, all they had to do was line up along the Kansas and Old Oklahoma borders . . . and wait. More than 100,000 land-hungry settlers gathered, all of them eager to claim as many plots of land as possible. On the fourteenth of the month, guns sounded, droves of people flooded the territory to stake their claims, and the "Greatest Run of the Century" began.[13]

It was on a first-come, first-served basis. The accounts of cheating, animal abuse, thievery, train robbery, bribery, deception, fraud, and killing make these people look like savages. But it was the gateway to the Promised Land. They would get to it no matter what it cost.

Horseback riders galloped ahead and set the prairies behind them ablaze to stop the walking masses; others tampered with railroad ties and train spikes to create accidents; officers welcomed bribes to let cheaters pass through. And when two or more settlers landed on the same plot at the same time, they often shot each other. Imagine this scene of ignorance and depravity. The Native Americans had been forced to hand over their prized land, which the European Americans had envied for many years. Now these white people were swarming like greedy children fighting over a single toy.

One immigrant group said, "We are glad to get back [home]. . . . We honestly would not take a claim in the new country as a gift now, after what we saw of the country and its people."[14]

In many ways, we are those same people with the same self-centered tendencies. Given the right circumstances, we'll act the same way, too. Today, however, the SimGospel plays an even larger, more global role. Advertising is everywhere and the SimGospel normalizes what seems like barbarism on the Cherokee Strip. Materialistic wealth and the normalizing of consumerism encourages and affords us every opportunity to indulge. It may look different than it did in 1893, but it is quite the same: cutting corners, ignoring neighbors, taking what we can, and collectively squashing with our self-righteous footprint.

If I seem to be exaggerating, think about how you would respond if a thief stole from you—a car from the garage, a promotion, a girlfriend, or your security (September 11, 2001). Hostility is the most common response. Yet, on a collective scale, we are stealing other people's adequate provision every time we take another acre that isn't rightfully ours. Every time we drive when we could walk, or hose down the sidewalk instead of sweeping it, or close our wallets when we could give out of our surplus (which is all of us in some form or another). Asking us to give it back seems like they are stealing from us. How odd is this?

When we hear of foreigners struggling due to lack, we are usually apathetic. By doing nothing except add another lock to secure our things, we imply, "Well, I don't know them, and in some ways they don't really exist in my world. Besides it's dog-eat-dog around here. Maybe they should just work harder." The SimGospel thrives on this attitude, and it doesn't have to exert much effort, because it knows we are most often in it for ourselves.

Apathy

In a college newspaper section called "The Roundtable," students offer their opinions regarding controversial issues. One particular edition asked, "What do you think of the recent bedbug problem on campus?" A junior majoring in criminal justice replied, "They weren't in our apartment, so it really didn't concern me." Is this someone who is ready to enter the justice world?

Yet even seeing the devastation of war or starvation or drought or genocide or other injustices rarely invokes more response than this. The SimGospel's me-centered focus and its pitiful treatment of others foster numbness when it comes to community. Bombings and hatred occur all over the world, but only when our own towers are hit in New York City do we suddenly concern ourselves with the world's terrorism problem.

In the documentary film *The Ad and the Ego,* there is a scene that made a strong impression on me. It shows gory bodies strewn about and heart-wrenching clips of the infirm in low-quality medical facilities during the first Gulf War. The film cuts to a news clip where Bryant Gumbel says, "Equally distressing is that, according to polls, 90 percent of the people really don't seem to be bothered by the fact that the government is censoring the images that they're getting." While the images continue to appear on screen, Jean Kilbourne says, "We didn't see those pictures, because that would be intolerable. But if you think of the people as objects, then violence becomes much more tolerable."[15]

What we don't know or cannot see won't crawl under our skin. We won't be reminded of the pain that exists all around us. The SimGospel promotes comfort, serenity, calm, and security. These painful images, however, tell us that our neighbors are experiencing a horror that we thought only existed in movies.

The close-up picture of a man's charred frame is nauseating. His face describes the terror and agony he felt while being burned to death. The bloated stomachs of dead or dying children cause us to say, "Thank God that my children don't have to live in such impoverished conditions." These images can make us sick, because they are real and we don't want to admit that they can happen. We think, "This kind of pain should not be in a serene and neighborly world." (Besides, it is hard to face guilt's haunting aroma when our cupboards reek of surplus.)

Apathy is a powerful form of violence to others. In appearance, though, it is often mild compared to 1893, and we are not as moved to consider our savagery. But whether savage or "civilized," being spoiled by wealth and provision leads to collective neglect, because we desire to remain undisturbed from our comfort.

As I close Parts I and II, I want to state the obvious—that the SimGospel and its liturgy, its idea of normal, have extensive effects on our identity, lifestyle choices, and care for others. But how do we step out of the fishbowl to differentiate between reality and false image? How do we make smaller footprints and see ourselves as stewards? How do we become agents of change and reference points for truth in building the kingdom of God?

We must learn how to live in the likeness of Christ.

Part III

Building the Kingdom . . . Together

8

Becoming like Christ

By now, we've seriously considered two questions: *Who am I?* and *Who is my neighbor?* In the light of advertising and the SimGospel message it notoriously carries, these questions are fundamental to moving forward. The answers to them point to the significance of bearing God's image—of seeing ourselves and others as we truly are. But, of course, the difference between recognition and action, and between knowledge and response to that knowledge, is large.

It is a gift to finally believe that God loves me. It is a sign of maturity to see that even when I fall under the poverty line in America, I am actually rich compared to most of the world. It is discernment to be able to name, with accuracy, how my workplace cuts corners, or how my course content lacks integrity with the school's mission. And it is a revelation of wisdom to hear between the waves of a radio ad and be able to separate fact from fiction, knowing that hair growth products are marketed to breed insecurity and that they fail to increase self-worth.

However, becoming like Christ is a movement from acknowledgment to activity. It is recognizing that we are extravagantly and supernaturally loved, and then allowing that gift to transform our daily lives. Ann Hagmann addresses this deep significance of being made in the image of God, but she also stresses the critical nature of living it out:

> It is not enough as a Christian to claim being made in our Creator's image; we are called to be conformed to the likeness of Christ. This is the hard part of the gospel where Jesus says we have to die in order to live, to pick up our cross and follow him, to seek first the kingdom of God and all else will be given to us.[1]

In this chapter, I will present two ways to help us move toward becoming like Christ: observing Jesus as the Ultimate Neighbor, and entering the body of Christ.[2]

The Ultimate Neighbor

Where is the truth?

Sylvia: What right do you have to take a baby and turn his life into some kind of mockery? Don't you feel guilty?

Christof: I have given Truman a chance to lead a normal life. The world—the place you live in—is the sick place. Seahaven is the way the world should be. . . . He can leave at any time. . . . If he was absolutely determined to discover the truth, there's no way we could prevent him. What distresses you, really, caller, is that ultimately Truman prefers his cell, as you call it.[3]

This dialogue is taken from the movie *The Truman Show*. It is about a television show where every person in the domed city of Seahaven is an actor, except for Truman. Truman Burbank doesn't know he is on television twenty-four hours a day. He has no clue that 5,000 cameras are strategically placed to watch his every move. He doesn't know there is a dome over Seahaven, and he doesn't know that weather, jobs, and family life are all controlled by a godlike man named Christof. Truman was put on this larger-than-life set as an infant, and he has never been off. He is the star who "gives hope and joy and inspiration to millions." And he doesn't have a clue.

In the movie, Christof (interesting name) is the show's creator. He is god in this staged world and acts as father to Truman, though Truman doesn't know he exists. Sylvia (of the dialogue above) was once an actress, but she fell in love with Truman and almost ruined the show. Christof fired her and now she sits at a real home, praying that Truman will discover the truth.

In midlife, Truman does begin to perceive that he is somehow on stage. He senses that the world acts in response to his actions, and it elicits suspicion and anxiety. As his quandary deepens, his "best friend," Marlon (another actor), sits down with him. Truman confesses, "Feels like the whole world revolves around me somehow." Marlon turns and says, "That's a lot of world for one man, Truman. Sure that's not wishful thinking?" Ironically, the world really does revolve around Truman, but it sounds like Marlon wishes he were in that role instead.

This film does a beautiful job describing the media's treatment of us. When we watch TV, we see actors at the center of attention. They are on the red carpet, they are chauffeured, and they have their own clothing lines. When I say that Jim Carrey plays Truman, it is most likely that you know exactly to whom I am referring. TV and the advertising it does make us aware of who we are or aren't compared to who or what is being advertised. It causes our perception of personal significance to be heightened.

Later in the movie there is an interview with Christof regarding Truman's suspicions. A correspondent asks, "Why do you think that Truman has never come close to discovering the true nature of his world until now?" Without skipping a beat, Christof replies, "We accept the reality of the world with which we are presented. It's as simple as that."

What a brilliant line! In the movie, Christof symbolizes the manipulator behind the SimGospel (a SimChrist to Truman, if you will). But to viewers like you and me, he is the truth-teller (a real savior to uncover the SimGospel). *The Truman Show* is a film that exaggerates the world "with which we are presented." The SimGospel captures our hearts and feeds us a dream life, but this movie exposes the simulation and causes us to shake our heads in disbelief. It provides one of those moments when we suddenly come to a halt in our thinking and realize that what we previously believed to be true is actually not.

I wonder how many of us have thought, "Yes, that movie really is a great depiction of Hollywood's effect on society, but I can't understand how people can be so foolish in the real world that they put faith in this fantasy," without ever thinking that we are not only susceptible but probably guilty of swallowing the same delusions. If Truman went his entire life not knowing, then who's to say that we haven't accepted "the reality of the world with which we are presented" as well?

What I am asking is this: how do we deconstruct a fabricated belief system that highlights our weaknesses, thrives off of our patronage, and neglects others?

If we are living in the likeness of Christ, then we should have a profound effect on the world. Our membership in a materialistic culture, care for others, and employment in places that ignore the work of building the kingdom should serve as a witness to the Gospel message. Knowing how to do these things, however, requires an active approach to learning. Like Truman eventually did, we must face the unknown and venture beyond what is comfortable and familiar in order to find the world outside of Seahaven.

Will the real Jesus please stand up?

Jesus: Unexpected servant

When bankers go through job training, they are taught to find counterfeit money by studying authentic bills. Studying what is real gives insight to what is not real, and it provides a benchmark for the standard by which all other dollars find validation. Here is where Jesus's life makes a worthy deposit, and it will do us well to see him as the model—the Ultimate Neighbor. Let us look at just four characteristics that validated Jesus's authenticity in ministry to others and service to God in heaven.

First and foremost, Jesus knew who and whose he was. In John 13:3, we read, "Jesus knew that the Father had put all things under his power, and that he had come from God and was returning to God."

Here was the Prince of Peace and King of Kings, and in the next statement this Dignitary washed the disciples' feet. Addressing the combination of dust, sandals, and smelly feet required humility, but knowing his identity allowed Jesus the freedom to do what others may have feared doing. The disciples obviously perceived this bold move. One of them even denied Jesus's offer. It was a job that certainly lacked public honor, so why was the Lord acting like a mere servant? Healthy identity freed him from bowing to vain cultural norms.

This level of health extended into his preaching as well. He was free in a way that could repel followers as quickly and effectively as he could draw them.

Imagine that you are a public speaker. Imagine that you are good enough to have people follow you like a celebrity. You arrive at the mall, and rumor gets out that you are down by the ice cream shop. A thousand shoppers cram into the main aisle begging for you to speak to them. Photographs flash like strobe lights, children crowd around asking for autographs, and the crippled manage their way to the front. They know you have healing power in your words. Fans hold signs that say, "You Rock!" and, "Tell us what our itching ears want to hear!"

How many of us at that ecstatic moment would climb atop the coin-operated spaceship ride and tell the crowd something that would have them throwing their signs, flipping us off, and dispersing in a matter of minutes? I know I wouldn't. I can hardly hold on to who I am or to whom I belong. I find myself persuaded by the crowd to fulfill and even exceed its expectations of me. I often place my identity in the defining hands of the onlookers, doing just what they want: telling them what their itching ears want to hear.

I have what Brennan Manning calls an imposter.[4] The imposter is a self-created image designed for public presentation. I keep it because it feeds my desire to continue playing the game. The rule is simple: I surrender truthful identity, and the imposter gives me the praises and acceptance of others in return.

While my imposter basks in the applause of the mall crowd, the SimGospel's idea of normal and its elusive cronies (all of the imposter's friends) stand over by the children's clothing store, encouraging and reinforcing. They are ever-present onlookers, always cheering and keeping my illusions alive.

Jesus's humility, however, kept him away from needing to be in the limelight. He was so caring for the crowd that he was beyond its popularity effects. Service was not about his being at the center. The disciples didn't expect this radical behavior, and neither do I. Until we move away from seeing ourselves as gods, we will not be able to conceive our being outside of the center or understand our role as caregivers. And there will be no washing of feet.

Jesus: Truth-teller

[H]is word is in my heart like a fire, a fire shut up in my bones. I am weary of holding it in; indeed, I cannot.

Jeremiah 20:9

Jesus saw behind the façade, and like Jeremiah, he could not keep silent. Jesus knew that the truth set people free whether they wanted to hear it or not. He didn't hold back in the face of opposition. Nor did he speak out in order to gain popularity. God had given him a charge, and to ignore it in any way would have been shortsighted. Jesus had a kingdom vision that carried him through the pressures of his culture, his followers, and his enemies.

I have always admired how he looked through people to see their needs. Telling the truth was Jesus's act of care—a way to address what the people most needed. For example, the disciples were fearful and often ignorant. Jesus knew they needed much growth before going out into the world, so he told them the truth, even if it was abrasive.

The Pharisees needed Jesus as well. They frequently missed the Old Testament's deeper significance, but Jesus understood the law outside of their cluttered definitions, and he wanted them to become healthy spiritual leaders. Of course, telling the truth threatened their system, but he cared for them and for the people they misled.

I can imagine the general public opposing Jesus's confrontation of the Pharisees. When someone has authority and respect, we often put him or her on a pedestal. Depending on our faith in them, any threat they receive is a threat to us as well. Jesus's threat to the religious practices of the day would have threatened the system these commoners so endorsed. As in the Wizard of Oz, it is fearful to look behind the curtain, because when falsehood is discovered, faith must deal with the shock. If Jesus were right, then it meant the Pharisees were wrong. If they were wrong, then what would happen to the people's faith?

With audacity, Jesus spoke to everyone in a way that made no excuses. He was concerned about a vision far greater than his ego. He was ushering in a kingdom that would require hard work, sacrifice, and even death to build. Telling the truth was the least he could do.

Jesus: Man of solitude

A third important facet of Jesus's model is solitude. Solitude is not simply being alone. As you may know, internal noise goes on regardless of crowd size. I've been at parties and experienced such quiet inside that it actually felt contemplative. On the other hand, I've been in the woods on a half-day solo hike and wished more than anything for a moment of silence from this kind of internal noise:

> How long do I have? What errands should I run when I get home? Why did he have to say that to me yesterday? I'm tired. And thirsty. Hey, when did I get a hole in my shoes? I'll need to buy another pair. I wonder who has good sales. Do I have enough money until I get paid? When is payday? Three . . . four . . . no, six days from now? Raises are due next month—maybe I can afford that new . . .

Sound familiar? With this level of racket, it is nearly impossible to hear what God is calling us to do.

Imagine a chalkboard already full of lecture notes and diagrams. You are looking at your own paper and trying to organize a few thoughts before class ends. You hear the professor say, "Don't forget the assignment on the board." You look up and scan from left to right through the clutter and search quickly for the page numbers: "What assignment? Is that a 41 or a 91?"

Now, think of the board as completely clean except for the assignment: You hear the professor say, "Don't forget the assignment I've written here." You look up and immediately see it, because it is all there is to see.

Jesus spent time with God, seeking direction, finding restoration, and gathering strength to endure the hard work before him (Matt. 14:23; Mark 1:35; Luke 6:12; 9:28; 22:41–44; John 17). It is quite a discipline to set time aside. It is even more difficult to achieve real solitude during that time. Henri Nouwen tells of an early Christian writer who describes the first stage of solitary prayer as the experience of a man who, after years of living with open doors, suddenly decides to shut them. The visitors who used to come and enter his home start pounding on his doors, wondering why they are not allowed to enter. Only when they realize that they are not welcome do they gradually stop coming.[5]

The noise of our own concerns and the worries that frustrate the silence not only block our communication with God, but also mask the assignments we are given to address our neighbors' needs. It is only when solitude is found that clarity allows the chalkboard of our minds to receive well.

There are many ways to achieve solitude, and certain methods are more effective for certain people. A simple and personal favorite of mine is reciting the Jesus prayer. The Jesus prayer came from the Eastern Orthodox church as early as the fifth century. In its most basic form it is simply, "Lord Jesus Christ, have mercy upon me."[6] However, other variations can be used: "Lord Jesus Christ, Son of the Living God, have mercy upon me, a sinner," or "Lord Jesus Christ, Lover of all, trail wide the hem of your garment—bring healing, bring peace." Whether sitting down for fifteen minutes on my porch swing, or driving to a conference, or walking to work in the morning, this prayer can be enjoyed.

One practice is to repeat the prayer, slowly and genuinely. Each time through, dwell specifically on one of the words or descriptions of God. The contemplative repetition encourages external noise to cease and creates a deeper silence with Jesus. Of course, heavier life concerns and longer periods of time away from prayer may make it seem impossible to come to this place. But regular and frequent practice (difficult for me) can not only help to quiet you but also allow you to know God better.

Jesus: Teacher

Finally, I want to look at Jesus's model of discipleship. He kept sharp partly by taking on the responsibilities of training and charging others to emulate him. If you have ever had to teach in any capacity, you may recall the proficiency it required. You may also remember the knowledge gained by spending time in research and preparation.

Tutoring an underclassman, showing a neighbor kid how to change the oil in a car, creating a lesson plan for student teaching, and leading a Sunday school class are all tasks that require being sharp in order for learning to take place. I cannot adequately explain how much I've learned in the process of writing this book, for example. But I have welcomed it, because I knew all the while that it was my act of worship, and that my integrity and your learning were at stake. I could not justify taking a haphazard approach for either of us.

Knowing that the possibility of another's formation is in my hands is nothing to grasp lightly. In fact, if the charge is taken without special care, it can quickly lead to abuse. When the teaching is of a religious nature, that abuse can be spiritual. But if it is handled with maturity and the fruits of solitude, it can draw others out of the fishbowl to a place where life is unveiled and the deceit of the SimGospel can fade.

If we claim to be carriers of the Gospel, we have a responsibility to teach through words and actions. When we do this, we proclaim what motivates us, and this form of witness points others to the truth. Jesus made this kind of proclamation vividly throughout his life, and he asks us to do the same.

In searching for the truth, studying Jesus's model is paramount. Being a *servant* to others strikes us, because it doesn't seem fitting for a king. However, this only strengthens his call for us to serve likewise. Being a *truth-teller* is significant, because it is based on care. He asks us to care genuinely, so that we won't withhold the healing truth from others.

Practicing *solitude* clashes with our fast-paced external and internal lifestyles. It was a customary discipline for him, but if it does not come easy to us, we ought to ask why. And being a *teacher* highlights our responsibility to be lifelong students. He was always teaching and always learning. If we are not always discipling and being discipled even in the mundane activities of life, then what are we doing with our time?

By observing this Ultimate Neighbor, we learn how to take being image bearers of God to another level. We learn how to live in the likeness of Christ. I want to highlight three practices that will be necessary for moving us along this path. They are studying scripture, learning from church history, and devoting ourselves to a healthy form of prayer. It is important that we consider their roles, for they are vital tools meant to equip us in countering the SimGospel's idea of normal. They are critical in strengthening us to withstand the SimGospel's debilitating message, and if we are faithful in exercising them, we will find ourselves appearing more and more like the Ultimate Neighbor, who is Christ.

Engaging with the text

We have just examined four characteristics of Jesus, but how is it that we know these? By engaging with the text. Studying Jesus as the model to follow is best learned by engaging in the stories where he plays lead character. Scripture is a reference point for healthy living. It is even the source for healthy living, and the more we study it, the better we will know how to apply it to the wounds of today's culture. Yet it requires discipline to set aside the time and space for comprehension.

With discipline, we will find ourselves clothed with the "full armor of God," complete with truth, righteousness, readiness, faith, salvation, and the Spirit, all of which we put on to stand against the devil's schemes (Eph. 6:11–17). Without it, we will subject his wisdom to the foolish whims of our human nature and lose real hope of combating the SimGospel.

The Bible is a very practical guide, filled with infinitely marvelous and also painful descriptions of life as God did and did not intend it. Scripture encompasses the great story of redemption, within which we are indeed blessed to have a part. It offers us a picture of the kingdom of God. It is the revelation of God's accompaniment with his people, and it is where we learn of his intentions, his patience, his justice, and his redemption through Jesus Christ. Furthermore, the way we as Christians engage with popular culture will succeed only if this same Word guides our vision for the kingdom:

> For the word of God is living and active. Sharper than any double-edged sword, it penetrates even to dividing soul and spirit, joints and marrow; it judges the thoughts and attitudes of the heart. Nothing in all creation is hidden from God's sight. Everything is uncovered and laid bare before the eyes of him to whom we must give account. (Heb. 4:12–13)

If the SimGospel hides, the Gospel reveals. If the SimGospel simulates hope, the Gospel fulfills. If the SimGospel dulls our senses, the Gospel makes us sharp. The Word of God is the vision that not only counteracts the SimGospel but far surpasses it as it is the model by which the SimGospel claims any substance in the first place.

I mentioned the Jesus prayer above, and how it can be used to accompany us into solitude and time with the Lord. Here, I've included a practical way to enter the scriptures.

For the past four or five years, I have served as a retreat director, using the spiritual exercises of St. Ignatius. St. Ignatius believed that entering scripture with our imagination and using all of the senses to experience the stories of Jesus's life was an excellent way to know Jesus more fully.[7] To begin, retreatants are encouraged to find a quiet place to pray, to sit in a posture that keeps them awake, and to spend a few minutes preparing themselves to be with God. Then they read a passage, such as Jesus's healing of the blind man, Bartimaeus, while considering the following questions: Who is in the scene? What does it smell like? How loud or dusty is it? What does Jesus look like, and what is he wearing? Pretending to be Bartimaeus, how do you feel when the crowd and Jesus are approaching? Pretending to be a disciple, how do you see Bartimaeus, the beggar? et cetera.

These are the kinds of questions that can reveal Christ's compassion to us. They can show his ability to listen and how he discerned the needs of others, even when surrounded by multiple demands. Also, this method can reveal the health status of a retreatant. Many times I have been told, "I couldn't enter the story at all. It was too noisy in my head. I was so frustrated that I just quit."

Engaging with the text is difficult work for most, if not all, of us, and it requires discipline to keep up with it. But practice and the help of the Spirit make it remarkably illuminating, especially regarding our wounds. The SimGospel puts a bandage over an infection, but scripture reveals the ways of the Great Physician. With wise use, we can know Jesus better and become agents of healing.

Words outside of the Word

Second, I want to suggest that we carefully read and study beyond the physical pages of the Bible. Christians often read current religious books to assist them in growing spiritually. We, including myself, read to understand Christian community and church worship; we read for tips on sharing the faith; we read as part of a Christian book study. However, beyond engagement with current material and scripture itself, we regularly neglect centuries of fine theological exposition and the historical development of the church as we know it today. We neglect to learn about the spread of the Gospel beyond Paul, Timothy, and other New Testament figures, about enthralling stories of martyrdom, and a multitude of other points that constitute the foundation the church stands on today.

Understanding scripture is not done only through reading scripture. Our pastors and priests give sermons and homilies that are scriptural but not exclusively consisting of words from God's Word. Postcanonical literature is full of God's continued work in the world and the Holy Spirit's ongoing revelation to us. For example, the concept of the Trinity wasn't named until the third century.[8] Should we dismiss this core element of theology because it wasn't spelled out with great clarity in the original text, but rather was unfolded centuries later?

Moreover, do we know the roots of our respective church traditions? Do we know when and by whom the Nicene and Apostles' creeds were written, and what it took for these statements to become realities? Discovering answers to some of these questions can spur our faith in mature directions. I, for one, realize that in writing this book I am not the first to create any of the material contained within it. I may use a few new terms, but recognizing that I follow 2,000 years of spiritual, cultural, and intellectual thought is quite humbling. I recognize my place and see that assuming the title *Student* is most fitting as a writer in the twenty-first century.

Engaging with the literature and teachings of church history will enable us to see patterns from other times and cultures. The Bible serves as the basis and primary reference point, but it is wise for us not to miss out on centuries of inspired teaching and faithful studying. Whether you agree with all of their theology or not, formative contributors such as Augustine (354–430), Thomas Aquinas (1225–1274), Martin Luther (1483–1546), John Calvin (1509–1564), and Karl Barth (1886–1968) are some of the major figures in church history. Reading their works can serve as good places to start.

Silence and the Word

Third, it is essential that we commit to the practice of prayer, which must be accompanied by silence and the Word. Above, I offered practical examples for reading scripture and finding solitude, but I want to emphasize the importance of these two elements coexisting. Henri Nouwen offers the following insight regarding scripture engagement. I think it is fitting, especially as it relates to the chalkboard metaphor:

Contemplative reading of the holy scriptures and silent time in the presence of God belong closely together. The word of God draws us into silence; silence makes us attentive to God's word. The word of God penetrates through the thick of human verbosity to the silent center of our heart; silence opens in us the space where the word can be heard. Without reading the word, silence becomes stale, and without silence, the word loses its recreative power. The word leads to silence and silence to the word. The word is born in silence, and silence is the deepest response to the word.[9]

In searching for the truth, how can we press forward without this principle at the heart of our movement? The "thick of human verbosity" includes everything from SimGospel sermons to the small voices in our heads that create confusion and worry. Prayer requires sound discernment.

Being quiet enough for long enough is surely difficult. But doing it for even fifteen minutes per day will provide the necessary space for discerning our role in a consumeristic culture. Of course, all disciples of Christ have the same general mission, but we each have specific job descriptions. Silence and the Word together offer clarity for discernment. With Jesus calling us to be in the world but not of it, prayer is essential. In *The Message*, Romans 12:1, 2, read as follows:

So here's what I want you to do, God helping you: Take your everyday, ordinary life—your sleeping, eating, going-

to-work, and walking-around life—and place it before God
as an offering. Embracing what God does for you is the best
thing you can do for him. Don't become so well-adjusted
to your culture that you fit into it without even thinking.
Instead, fix your attention on God. You'll be changed from
the inside out. Readily recognize what he wants from you,
and quickly respond to it. Unlike the culture around you,
always dragging you down to its level of immaturity, God
brings the best out of you, develops well-formed maturity
in you.[10]

How do I give him these parts of my life? How can I "recognize what he wants"? How should I "quickly respond to it"?
Paying attention, changing, thinking—these are processes,
not destinations. And they require patience through the hard
work of prayer and silence. God's voice will get lost in the din
of our own noise if we are not careful. Once this happens, it
is very easy to convince ourselves of knowing God's will, even
though we may not have a clue what it really is!

If every situation requires decision making, and every decision requires wisdom; and if wisdom requires spiritual discernment, and discernment requires a basis, then in order to be
faithful as Christians, our basis must be the Word. Furthermore, if the Word is the antithesis of the SimGospel, and the
SimGospel disrupts wisdom with noise, then in order to be
servants to our neighbors, we must clear the air. Silence and
the Word are critical in becoming like our Ultimate Neighbor,
Jesus.

But how do we keep from convincing ourselves wrongly
of God's will? Enter: community. In searching for truth, we
can watch and study Jesus, and we can develop healthy individual practices to grow spiritually. But the large body of
people around us plays a significant role in guiding, caring,
shaping, and sharing. Together, we can move well toward the
truth and toward becoming Christians who speak prophetically into the culture.

The body of Christ

Healthy neighbors

Imagine not just one Ultimate Neighbor, but 10 or 10,000! What love would be proclaimed! What problems would be addressed! If only we all responded to God's call to live in the likeness of Christ. But we don't. And we never have.

Someday, however, we will. Until then, we should put one foot in front of the other, surrounding ourselves with as much wisdom and support as possible. Nouwen understood the importance of gathering resources in this manner, and he knew that our weaknesses would protrude and inflict damage if they were not held accountable. The "word and silence both need guidance," he said. "How do we know that we are not deluding ourselves, that we are not selecting those words that best fit our passions, that we are not just listening to the voice of our own imagination?"[11]

Well, we don't know these things, and that is why we need community. Removing distortions is a task for multiple eyes and ears. Unfortunately, it is hard work to settle into, as is even finding a good community. And while being in one is a prerequisite for individual health, the body of Christ is sometimes a difficult place to be.

The closer we get to knowing others intimately, the deeper the wounds go when they are inflicted. Moreover, the lonelier our hearts become when outcast, and the colder we turn when betrayed. On the flip side, however, the closer we get to knowing others intimately, the deeper we can know ourselves. As well, the greater we can return love to others, and the more clearly we can see God's presence in our lives. We need community to speak divine truth about who we are, whether this is difficult or not.

Richard Gula believes that "love is the relational force that enhances our sense of being somebody, of being persons of dignity and worth. In the way we treat others, we can help

157

them claim for themselves what is already theirs."[12] By loving others, we proclaim that God is a relational Being and that we are loved by him. But we need others in order for this to occur. We need others through relationships to act as visible and tangible reminders of who, and whose, we are. We are communal by nature and called to the same simply because we are made in his image.

If "being the image of God is irreversible,"[13] then we need to acknowledge the ways we underestimate the fullness of this mystery. If it is irreversible, then what are those things that keep us from believing it? In other words, no matter what we have been told or how the truth has been abused, the dignity and worth of being God's image bearers remain intact. We may not see it or believe it, but it is an undeniable reality. Personally, I want community to help me dig through the superficial layers to find it.

This is where we must be willing to accept what our ears are not itching to hear. The SimGospel has great power in distorting the truth. First it creates shortcomings and flaws. Then it encourages us to be dissatisfied with them. Then it offers easy, empty paths to enlightenment and fulfillment.

The multiple sets of eyes and ears in healthy community will help us navigate safely through this simulation, and on the way we will discover Christ among us.

The church

Community can be formed with a friend, a mentor, a small group, a bowling team, an office staff, or even an author's words in print. Yet scripture claims that the best source of community is the body of Christ. The church is a particular parish, a congregation down the street, and the prophets and teachers before, during, and after Christ's life. It is where truth is sought, and where accountability is present. It is a group of people who attempt to move together spiritually and who recognize that unity is founded in Christ's redemptive work on the cross.

This body functions, challenges, and reveals through the work of the Holy Spirit. It is where we frequently catch glimpses of God and grapple with the grace that tows us in by love. It tends to be a place where God is permitted entrance. Here, he reminds us of who we really are, and he forgives us for the acts of treason we commit every time we invest faith in the temporal teachings of the SimGospel.

The body of Christ is not a place or thing to be viewed as a marketplace, where we come to purchase goods and pleasures. Our goal is not to *get something out of it*. Rather, we are to give ourselves as gifts (getting something out of it is a by-product). By investing and creating hospitality, we receive the gifts of others in return. In chapter 6, I said that through hospitality, we see the characteristics of God. The better we see God, the more potential we have for building a community that accurately reflects his hopes for us.

The apostle Paul urges the early church to consider living this out:

> Each one of us has a body with many parts, and these parts all have different uses. In the same way, we are many, but in Christ we are all one body. Each one is a part of that body, and each part belongs to all the other parts. We all have different gifts, each of which came because of the grace God gave us. The person who has the gift of prophecy should use that gift in agreement with the faith. Anyone who has the gift of serving should serve. Anyone who has the gift of teaching should teach. Whoever has the gift of encouraging others should encourage. Whoever has the gift of giving to others should give freely. Anyone who has the gift of being a leader should try hard when he leads. Whoever has the gift of showing mercy to others should do so with joy. (Rom. 12:4–8 NCV)

When each of us gives in ways that we are able, and when we do it well, community begins to take shape as a reflection of the kingdom. This kingdom offers shelter, healing, and guidance, which serve the rest of our world as a reference point for goodness.

Being like the Ultimate Neighbor and being part of the body of Christ—these require action, but not just any action. They require wise, diligent, humble action. When we show these attributes, the world will see our great witness of the Gospel and be encouraged to find hope in something other than product consumption and keeping up with the Joneses.

Becoming a SimGospel Heretic

A democratic civilization will save itself only if it makes the language of the image into a stimulus for critical reflection—not an invitation for hypnosis.

Umberto Eco[1]

We have just spent time looking at reference points for health. These elements are not always easy to attain, but then again, they aren't "products" being marketed as quick fixes either. This is something we must accept. Becoming like Christ requires discipline, patience, counsel, and an approach that counteracts the SimGospel's methodology. Interestingly, the more we become like Christ, the more we become *heretics* of the SimGospel.

This chapter begins with a few words about discernment and ends with a call for the kind of faith heretics need. Sandwiched in the middle is a hefty portion of practical suggestions and activities for you to use.

It is difficult to spend quality time in the scriptures, because it is so much easier to do other activities that catch our attention. Watching TV, reading magazines, and listening to the radio are a few of them. We spend most of our time on the couch with a remote, or going out on Fridays to see the newest movies, or sitting at coffee shops while poring through popular magazines. We often awake to music stations and have the CD player come on automatically when we start the car. These are easy things because they are often inviting, seductive, distracting, consoling, formative, and even addictive and they take so little effort on our part.

What would it look like if before we cut back on our time spent on these activities, we began engaging critically with their content—with the stuff we're actually digesting? This way, after serious critique, we could make educated and theologically sound decisions regarding what to condone or how to back off.

"'Everything is permissible'—but not everything is beneficial" (1 Cor. 10:23). This statement does not license me to go wild or to abandon self-censorship. It is about discernment. There are movies, for example, that I personally avoid, not because they lack redemptive elements, but because I know they would not benefit my health. Yet, before I write them off, I think about why.

An R-rated movie may offer great truths about how we ought to live, or about how God intends for us to serve him and his people. *The Green Mile* [2] and *Dead Man Walking* [3] are two on my favorites list. For some people, however, these films would not be beneficial to watch. They are difficult movies, and I do not recommend that anyone sees them without careful consideration and discernment. But they benefit me because they serve as powerful contemporary metaphors for Jesus's work on the cross.

My intention is not to make a case for R-rated films or to hand out a pop-culture license to be spiritually ignorant. This is about discerning the ideas and belief systems that are advertised in all forms of media, whether in G-rated movies, where the apparently harmless content disarms us, or in *Cosmopolitan* magazine, which numbs us in the grocery line. Everything we watch or listen to requires active discernment before being considered beneficial.

God calls us to be SimGospel heretics, which demands attention and prayer and telling the truth. In community, we ought to be helping each other in this quest to unveil what keeps the world from seeing Christ. Eco's words, quoted above, are helpful to us. He reminds us that we are to be about critical reflection and not hypnosis. Certainly, it is easier to have media as background noise or as something to veg out on, but if we want the world to look different, then we have to think and act differently.

Commercial development

To open this next piece on practical application, I have included two short stories. They are reminders of how complex and intentional the ad world is, and I hope they elicit an equally serious response.

I was visiting a friend in Hollywood, and we ended up as extras in a TV commercial. The first day took place on a golf course, and we were among a hundred or so people to be used as ambience. For eight hours, we were placed and rearranged per the director's request. Before we went home, however, he lined us up so that he could see us. "We are going to shoot a more detailed scene tomorrow, and we only need ten of you," he announced. Then he and the producer stood together and began a hushed dialogue about us. They motioned and nodded and carefully picked us out one by one, like captains picking teams for grade-school kickball. Ninety extras were sent away.

163

It was my beard that secured a spot, but I told them I couldn't return unless my friend came. We got spots nine and ten. While I felt strangely honored to be chosen (Hollywood hype, I suppose), but I could not help feeling like a commodity, a product among many, with my beard leaning out from the shelf, vying for attention and announcing that I was different from the others. In the end, I was worth the purchase. We were adjectives selected to modify the $3 item behind this commercial.

The following day, the ten of us milled around a set from dawn to dusk. There with us was a lighting crew, director, producer, make-up artist, a camera crew, technical assistants, a set manager, errand boys, a sound crew, a double for the golf pro from the day before, and a gourmet chef with his staff to cater our meals (about thirty-five people total). It was quite an experience, and it all existed for a mere seven seconds of footage. Seven seconds to watch a white-gloved hand (allegedly that of the golf pro) reach into a pouch of her golf bag to grab a bottle of vitamins. I stood in the background with the extras, clapping gently as if a great putt had been made. No dialogue, no golf swings—just a hand, a bottle, and the background effect of a large crowd. I was dumbfounded by the amount of time, money, energy, and talent that went into seven seconds of a soon-to-be-forgotten commerical.

My second story begins with a phone call from a telemarketer. He told me he was conducting a survey for marketing reasons and asked if I would participate. I said yes. A few days later, a VHS tape came in the mail with instructions. I put it in the VCR and watched a thirty-minute proposed sitcom (the video was self-erasing, so it could be watched only once) and then answered a series of questions about products we use in our home. The following day, I called the telemarketer back, per his request.

The man instructed me to reinsert the video in order to watch the remaining twenty seconds, which was a commercial for Gillette shaving cream. For the next forty-five minutes, I was drilled with dozens of questions. First about the sitcom:

What kind of shows do I watch? Do I think I'd watch this show again? Was the show funny? Who was my favorite character? Why was he my favorite? And so on. Then I endured a barrage of questions (many more than for the sitcom): Do you use Gillette products? A: Never. B: Sometimes. C: Always. . . . How old are you? Do you shave? Would you use this Gillette product? Would you use it in the morning? How smooth is it? Do you think it should be flavored? What physical characteristics of the actor in the commercial do you remember? And so on. I finally laughed and asked my inquisitor if he was serious. He didn't know how to respond, because his only job was to gather prespecified information from potential consumers like me—not to joke outside of his script.

The advertising company he represented wanted to know *everything*, and I learned that not one second or element of the completed Gillette ad would be accidental. This is the kind of effort that goes into all ads. Motions, color, hairstyles, sound, the number of people and how they make facial expressions, leaf colors, water reflections, bran-flake positions and milk splashes—all of these are advertisement pieces chosen carefully or acted out through a tedious, intentional process.

Amazing, isn't it? An entire industry working overtime to construct and expand a consumer culture. In light of this, I want to recommend four media guides who can sharpen our senses, increase our understanding, and mobilize us to action. When we consider their wisdom, they too become "members" of our community. It is certainly good to understand the SimGospel and our Christian responsibilities on a theoretical plane, but we must take action. Reading is an excellent place to start.

Media guides

1. Jean Kilbourne has already been mentioned several times. I will say as my friend said to me, "If you read *Can't Buy My Love: How Advertising Makes Us Think and Feel,* you will

never look at advertisements the same way again."[4] Kilbourne is the guru of advertising critique. Awarded Lecturer of the Year twice by the National Association of Campus Activities, she has been thinking about the destructive power of advertising for decades. She pays special attention to alcohol and tobacco ads, and the negative effects of advertising on women's body image.

2. *Eyes Wide Open: Looking for God in Popular Culture* is an excellent guide to seeing media from a Christian perspective.[5] Author William D. Romanowski is a professor of communication arts and sciences at Calvin College. In this book, he challenges readers to engage with what we spend so much intentional and unintentional time doing. He believes that media is rarely a random expression. Rather, it is an art form and message board, full of symbolism, stories, and viewpoints. Film producers, he would say, are artists in the same way that painters are artists. He suggests that great insight can be gained when we ask good questions such as, What ideas are being presented? and How are characters portrayed through interaction, emotion, and appearance?

3. Chuck Colson was advisor to President Nixon, indicted in the Watergate scandal, and later became a Christian while in jail. His daily commentary, *BreakPoint,* challenges Christians to see the importance of applying the Gospel to all spheres of life.[6] He believes that when Christians do not engage in the transformation of financial institutions, education systems, health fields, etc., they pose no threat to the dominant cultural ideas and practices.

In essence, he asks, "Where will the Lordship of Christ be manifested if the people of God separate themselves from dialogue about, and response to, those ideas and practices?" This reminds me of what Paul demonstrated in Athens: he didn't keep his awareness of dominant secular behavior to himself, and he didn't stay secluded in the comfort of his church group. He was neither ignorant nor inactive. Colson does likewise. He demonstrates his passion for intersecting

Gospel truths with everything from prison reform to best sellers, from pornography to Washington politics.

4. Obviously, there is an abundance of resources that would serve well as media guides, but I will mention only one more in detail. It is *Critique: Helping Christians Develop Skill in Discernment*,[7] edited by Denis Haack. *Critique* is a thoughtful and relevant newsletter/magazine with a mission "to call attention to resources of interest to discerning Christians; to model Christian discernment; and to stimulate the people of God to think biblically about all of life and culture."

Eve's Revenge, by Lillian Calles Barger, *Unfettered Hope,* by Marva Dawn, *How Much Is Enough?* by Arthur Simon, *Reaching Out,* by Henri Nouwen, *Amusing Ourselves to Death,* by Neil Postman, *The High Price of Materialism,* by Tim Kasser, and *No Logo,* by Naomi Klein are just a few other helpful Christian and non-Christian voices. They all have Christian things to say, which is why they are important as guides to engagement with a culture so pervaded by the SimGospel.

The following activities are presented to accommodate a number of learning and teaching styles. Consider them as tangible ways to respond to the SimGospel. I've arranged them in three main categories, though they can easily overlap: private practice, public action, and group activities.

Private practice

Last night, I watched a reality TV show while my wife ran a few errands. Of course, the temptation with this genre is to be entranced by the drama, action, suspense and up-close emotional reactions of the contestants, but I don't watch these shows often, which makes it seem easier to stay disconnected. I found it helpful to mute the television during commercial breaks and ask myself a few questions:

- How is background music used? Do I even notice it? How would the show change without it, especially in the part where they name who is staying and who is leaving the show?

- Why are contestants on the show in the first place? How strong is their desire for recognition and "being known"?
- Why do I feel privileged to view the periodic side interviews with individual contestants? Can I really be on the "inside" when a million others are watching too?

Later in the episode, I turned my attention to the ads, asking why and how they were placed in this particular time slot. Advertisers want to create a seamless program between ads and showtime, and I believe that when we separate them, it keeps our senses sharp.

Here is something you can do when reading a magazine: ask yourself whether a particular advertisement corresponds with the magazine's content. For instance, a fitness magazine may have a beer ad showing an athlete (in action) with a six-pack symbol superimposed on his abdomen. Or, you may see something like what I found in *Family Fun* magazine. A woman is sitting on the end of the couch, smiling and reading the newspaper. Her three children are on the other end, fully and individually engrossed in handheld games run by RadioShack batteries. Two of the kids are wearing headphones. The ad says, "Hear that? It's the sound of silence. . . . For this kind of peace, we should win a humanitarian award." Is this what *Family Fun* magazine represents? Silencing family members with electronic devices in order to escape?

Another idea is to curb your weekly dose of television (or whatever is your most frequently enjoyed medium). Instead of two hours, cut to one; instead of five nights, cut to three. More radical, but very useful, is to turn off the TV for a period of time. I said earlier that my wife and I went without it for five years. It may be too difficult to quit cold turkey, and I'm not convinced it is even necessary, so just try one month, or fast from TV during Lent. An interesting result is that the longer you abstain from watching, the more you will forget what is showing on what nights, which lowers anticipation to catch the following episodes. Perhaps a more important result is that commercials take on a see-through dimension when you've been away from them. You may have a reaction like, "Commercials just seem stupid to me now. How do they expect me to buy into that garbage?" At this point, it is important to ask yourself why you feel that way. You may be surprised by the clarity of your insights.

Public action

Obviously there are many things we can practice as individuals, but taking public action—even as an individual—can have lasting benefits. Participate in "TV-Turnoff Week."[8] Or send a letter to any magazine that shows *dis*integration between their content and endorsements. It's a simple act but it makes a strong statement, especially if they include your comments in the letters to the editor.

Protect "ad-free" zones. For instance, my three-year-old watches *Sesame Street* and a couple of other programs on the local PBS station. (As an adult, perhaps you watch *The Charlie Rose Show* or *Frontline*.) Because it is public broadcasting, it is supposed to be ad-free, and I like this fact because Emma cannot be targeted by advertisers. When PBS says, "Thank you to the Such-n-Such Foundation," I know that this generic acknowledgment has no impact on her. However, when sponsorships by corporations like McDonald's, Chuck E. Cheese, and Frosted Flakes land in this ad-free zone and commercialize their own endorsements, I take serious notice. There are plenty of public spaces open for branding, and PBS isn't one of them.

You can also subscribe online to an organization like Commercial Alert, which provides regular notices on justice issues related to media. Links and formatted letters (to governing officials, etc.) allow you to easily support or protest specific issues. My letter to PBS took five minutes, which encourages me to act more often.[9]

Do these actions make a difference? Well, when Major League Baseball officials teamed up with Columbia Pictures to promote the release of *Spider-Man 2* with ads on infield bases, one man started an online petition. His list filled immediately, and the public outcry caught the attention of ESPN. ESPN, in turn, polled 45,000 people (mostly sports fans) to see what they thought. Remarkably, 79.4 percent strongly opposed the idea, stating that it was important to preserve ad-free space. Indeed, it was preserved.[10]

Can you start an online poll?

Group activities

Reading and thinking and acting publicly on your own are great ways to begin, but inviting one or more people to join you generates many more ideas and helps to steer misaligned thinking. Of course, including others can easily happen with a stranger in the airplane seat next to you. It can also take place in the break room when you play the devil's advocate with a few colleagues, but here I will offer a couple more organized ideas. Hopefully, by moving together with a group of people, you will all become more publicly active. For example, you can all participate in "TV-Turnoff Week."

The first idea is similar to a private practice I mentioned above, except that I suggest recording the TV commercials during a prime-time show. Invite a friend or small group to analyze them with you. Start by watching the ads. Determine what product is being sold, and describe objectively what is taking place. Then watch them again and take note of prevalent details and messages, particularly when the ads are for alcohol or beauty products. What is really being sold? Try to determine what basic human need is being used to carry the product and what the company is promising. The following questions should encourage your thinking and generate discussion:

- Why are these particular ads placed within this particular program?
- Who is the target audience? If me, how am I being defined? Young, old, educated, pleasure-seeking, incompetent?
- What values are present?
- How are women treated? And men?
- How are relationships depicted?
- What role do neighbors play? Do they represent a fabricated standard? Do they serve as the Joneses? Are they disregarded or treated without dignity?
- Imagine the ad summarized and delivered from a pulpit. What is the SimGospel's sermon content?

I have offered two lightly critiqued examples below to demonstrate what you may discover when you take ads seriously. One is a TV commercial, and the other is a billboard I saw while driving through Chicago.

In the TV commercial, a father is sitting on the couch with his two daughters, who appear to be between nine and thirteen years old. Seated in a chair at the end of the couch, as you might see in a traditional psychiatrist office, is a salesman. The father comments to the salesman that his girls have been "like this for some time."

A cell phone on the coffee table rings, and like cats pouncing, both girls attack the phone, each trying to answer it before the other can. They roll viciously on the floor and throw each other across the room, fighting, screaming for command, and yelling to the caller. The exaggerated display is oddly humorous.

After a few more blows to each other, the camera pans back to the two men. The salesman recovers from what he has just seen and says to the dad, "I'm pretty sure we can help." The scene closes and the company name Sprint appears on a black screen.

After seeing this commercial, here are some thoughts I might contribute in a group setting. The first, and most observable, is that this family's living space resembles a psychiatrist's office. Thus, the salesman is put in the position of a highly trained professional. He is there to offer counsel. Many parents struggle to raise their kids, especially in the preteen and teenager years. There is no magic formula to attain peace and quiet, and they aren't sure how to reason with their increasingly independent children. In many ways, parents hunger for counsel to dispel the endless chaos. Of course, Sprint knows this, so they send an *expert*.

Interestingly, the expert comes to the aid of a father, not a mother. Fathers stereotypically have no clue how to raise children, particularly girls. If the salesman had come to help a mother, it would have been terribly insulting. But, for some reason, men are okay with being labeled "incompetent." (Consider the slogan for a Dodge Caravan ad: "Gets more done than most husbands.")

What sits most awkwardly with me, though, is the commercial's strong value judgment. According to the ad, it is not important to teach children good communication skills, or how to negotiate, compromise, or share. It dismisses these fundamental community elements. What we see instead are *instant solutions to life's complex problems*.[11] "Buy this phone option and your children's care for each other will become heavenly. Consult with Sprint, and we'll counsel your obvious dysfunction."

Well, what happens when these girls become women who enter college and have to share a room with a stranger? Without formative models for living in community, it is likely that they will quarrel in much the same way.

I want to add that I cannot claim personal exemption from the ad's influence. Of course, it is only one isolated commercial. It made me laugh, but that's about it. And I'm not interested in new phones or innovative phone options for my family. Therefore, I have no vested interest that warrants paying much attention to it. So, what effect could it possibly have on me?

In the documentary *The Ad and the Ego,* various media professionals are interviewed, and at one point, their comments are linked to make the following strong statement:

"People's experience of advertising is not sort of one ad by itself, each at a time, but rather advertising begins to sort of constitute a totality for people, it becomes an environment." "Because it's pervasive, it's taken for granted. We don't see it very well because we're surrounded by it in multiple media all the time from the time we're born to the time we die." "They're so around us. They're so much a part of our environment that we don't even think about them." "Advertising as a totality repeats certain kinds of consistent messages again and again and again." "The average American is exposed to over 1,500 ads every day. Now, of course, we don't pay attention to all of those ads, but the effect of advertising is cumulative, and it's mostly unconscious." "It's like breathing the air. You don't notice the pollution."

What effect does this one Sprint commercial have? Perhaps little, but ads insert vocabulary and meanings into a language we use to interact with each other. With this language, we convey messages across our culture. Viewers at home hear it, their children's friends at school reinforce it, the viewers go to work and build it, and the children go out and buy it. Then the children become professors and teach it, and the cycle continues.

Engagement with even this one commercial is essential. It is only a thirty-second clip, but I see clues in it that point to the larger advertising environment, and this affects all of us deeply.

The second ad is a billboard I saw in Chicago. On the right is a sporty Nissan Maxima. On the left is the text, "The meek shall inherit the passenger's seat." I get it. And my familiarity with the biblical reference grabs my attention. Religious themes in advertising often elicit greater consideration from me, and I wonder if Nissan assumes that I am acquainted with Matthew 5:5.

173

Whether I know scripture or not, the passenger's seat in a consumeristic culture is undesirable (remember the other Nissan ad in chapter 5?). Meanwhile, the driver is given power, control, and ownership. Meekness is mocked, consigned to the hapless passenger. Who wants to emulate the follower?

Yet when I think of the meek as humble, patient people, I do want to emulate them. Nissan uses the word out of context, and the meek get disregarded. Ironically, the meek are those who would actually care for the ad designers who demean them. They are also the type who would insist on being passengers—and backseat ones at that! Having power over others would have no value to them. Instead, the ad is geared toward people who struggle with second place and whose "imposters" are active. But what about others who are neither honorably meek nor heavily imposter-driven? Personally, I still hear the ad announce that meekness is undesirable and that ownership and power are more important.

Discussing ads with others is always beneficial, because it invites differing perspectives. What you see and hear may be different than what your friend or small group perceives, and this leads to more thoughtful critique. Another method for engaging with television ads is to watch them without sound. Consider these questions for your group:

- What do you think the voice-over is saying? What kind of music might be playing?
- How is the ad designed visually? Why bright blues or subtle grays? Why those specific actions?
- What do physical gestures say about relationships between characters?

Now replay the same ad(s) with sound, but close your eyes:

- What background noises are there? How does the sound compare/contrast with that of an amateur family video?

- Would the ad be effective if it could only be heard and not seen?
- If you've seen the ad before, is it possible to only listen, or do you see it playing in your mind?

A few years ago, two student leaders and I led a weekly discussion group. On one occasion, Matt cut out ten ads from a variety of popular magazines and then covered the name brands, including any revealing information, and laid them on the table. Each participant had to answer two questions for every ad: "What is being used to sell the product? (Be specific—don't just say 'sex.')" and, "What product is being sold?" Afterwards, everyone shared their answers, including why. It led to a wonderful conversation, and I've used the activity several times since.

For a specifically scriptural approach, pick a season on the church calendar and its accompanying Bible passages.[12] Facilitate a short-term Bible study—maybe six weeks—that compares and contrasts the Christian faith with the belief systems laced through popular advertising. A rather obvious example would be combining Advent with holiday season ads before Christmas. We talk every year about the "reason for the season," but most of us pay little attention. Perhaps meeting at a restaurant *in* the local mall would provide a curious environment—how does it feel to study scriptures about Christ's birth when you're surrounded by the clamor of commercialization?

You can try a more theatrical idea by splitting the group into subgroups of three or four. Provide a make-believe brand name and a slogan. Assign a different genre to each group (radio, billboard, TV . . .), and give them ten minutes to be the marketing team for an advertising agency whose job is to create an effective ad. When everyone is finished, have each group present. It is fun to do and funny to watch. As an observer/facilitator, notice similarities and differences between their homemade ads and those in popular media. Then ask the participants about what you saw. I found this activity in

175

the curriculum guide for the documentary *The Ad and the Ego*. The guide may be difficult to locate, but it is worth the search. *The Ad and the Ego* is an excellent, provocative critique of pop-culture advertising.[13]

One last example, to which I'll add some thoughts: facilitate a Sunday education class on body image and image bearing. This idea could be used to promote cultural discernment skills in church. By using scripture and popular magazines to show truth and distortions, community members will be able to see practical application of the Gospel in places where it is usually absent.

Unfortunately, in Christian education we often gravitate toward what we might consider *holy* at the expense of avoiding the *unholy*. This often causes us to shy away from the activities above. Meanwhile, we surround ourselves at home with the very stuff that we think is too unholy to bring to church. We talk about the unholy as if it were something separate from us and then criticize those who glorify it. But when the holy has something tangible to illuminate, it testifies to the power of the Gospel.

At a Christian conference for university students, the speaker was sharing examples of how we trade God's love for surrogate loves. He talked about Mother Teresa: the amazing gifts she brought to humanity, her humility, and the dignity and reverence others have for her. Then he opened a Victoria's Secret catalog and talked about the models. He talked about beauty and God's creation and how these women were also image bearers like Mother Teresa.

So far we had been listening, but now we were eager to see how he would connect it all. Then, he shocked us by presenting a picture on the large screen. It was a cropped photo of a Victoria's Secret model's body with the head of Mother Teresa. Though it received appalling responses from most, it was exactly the response he hoped for. He wanted the audience to feel the disparity between the two images now formed into one.

Folks called out, "That's just wrong!" And it seemingly was.

"But why?" he asked.

"It's degrading to Mother Teresa," they cried. "We don't want to think of Mother Teresa physically. She is valued by what she did, not by what she looked like." Others said, "Victoria's Secret models don't live like her; they're just models. We can't say that they have less worth, but next to Mother Teresa, they just don't seem as real, or as important."

The connection was made. It was clear that our pharisaical approach had embraced Mother Teresa but neglected the wayward models. Don't we do this every day though? Even if we don't receive the lingerie catalog in the mail, we condone, without critique, the same kind of disparity every time we absorb a magazine or thoughtlessly peruse while waiting in the checkout line. We never think *dignity* or *no dignity*. We just don't think. We objectify (adjective-fy) the model and thank God for the saint. This kind of differentiation, however, highlights the SimGospel's effects on our understanding of being image bearers and our indifference to its presence in the world. It was a poignant example that revealed our need for a pop-culture conversion.

We need to be a participative community that not only thinks but also seeks what wholeness really is. With multiple eyes and ears, we can hone our engagement skills and bear witness to the Gospel. Collectively, we can serve our neighbors by exposing the SimGospel. But in order to act like heretics, we must confront ease. We need Jesus the Servant and Truth-teller; we need media guides and the body of Christ to challenge us in countercultural ways.

As a campus minister, I feel this challenge all of the time. I know students who find their worth in status symbols (including what they *will* have after getting a good job). I can't avoid these folks or simply tell them to stop behaving immaturely. And I can't condone their behavior by sitting by without ever engaging them on this issue. However, I can see that they are questioning where to find worth. I must love them as my neighbors just as Christ loves me.

Situations like these are excellent means for me to look carefully, seek to understand, and get a peek behind the façade. If I can determine where the empty answers are coming from and from where they are being sought, I can respond by actively caring as Christ cares. But if I don't engage and ask questions, I may never be effective in SimGospel territory. I can share the Gospel and encourage church attendance or Bible study, but I can't stop there. If I don't help others navigate through the façade that the SimGospel and advertising perpetuates, it will be terribly difficult to help them out of the mind-set that excluded Christ in the first place.

In order to become SimGospel heretics, we must participate actively with others and invite the wisdom of the community to sharpen us. We must "take captive every thought to make it obedient to Christ" (2 Cor. 10:5). God has instilled in us a vision of the kingdom, and we've been given the choice to merely observe or to wisely engage. The test is whether or not we'll choose to engage.

A leap of faith

Trust: A rare commodity

Sometimes we refrain from heretical action because we feel inadequate. Sometimes it is because we are ignorant. But often, and this seems to be supported by the fact that we affirm the SimGospel's promises, it is a matter of faith. We believe these glamorous promises even though we know they are full of holes. So why do we stake our claim in this empty form of religion? For me, the answer is simple: it is tangible and offers immediate gratification and instant solutions. It is simple and readily available, and I can follow its guidelines by my own strength and resources. There is no unknown element, and it is easy to communicate because it is popularly accepted.

On the other hand, Christianity works on the basis of a more risky faith. Christianity requires us to invest in the unknown, and this is murky business. There is a fear regarding what lies beyond the familiar and comfortable, and we rarely venture toward it with any measure of confidence. Yet I believe true freedom exists there.

Perhaps lack of trust has something to do with it. In the movie *Indiana Jones and the Last Crusade,* there is a climactic scene after Indiana's father has been shot. In order for his father to receive healing, Indiana has to obtain the Holy Grail. But first he must answer a series of riddles that will guide him through various death traps. The final challenge occurs at a lion statue where the path falls away into a bottomless pit. The door he needs to enter is on the other side of this dark abyss, and there is no foreseeable way to cross. The riddle states, "Only in the leap from the lion's head will he prove his worth."[14]

Here is the biggest risk of all, and Indiana realizes that it requires a leap of faith. It is a step into the unknown, and the challenge is laden with fear and impossibility. He stands erect, closes his eyes, and slowly leans forward with one foot. As viewers, we are anxious. Like Indiana, we have no idea what will happen. He steps out . . . and then lands on an invisible walkway! Just when there appeared to be no other way to save his father, the unforeseeable happened.

Faith is the bedrock of our relationship with God. Somehow we must listen for God's voice and then trust him to lead us into the unknown. The SimGospel is so tempting because it is easy. The Gospel, however, demands courage and trust. Without faith we will never leap from the lion's head. We will have to count our losses and try to find contentment in other unfulfilling ways this side of salvation.

Under the claws of the Caregiver

Surrendering ourselves to God's mercy is often very difficult. Will he come through? Will he show me the way? Will he fill my deepest longings? These are real questions that accompany real doubt. Because the SimGospel is based on immediate, albeit temporary, gratification, we are accustomed to getting results *now*. Consequently, we find it nearly unbearable to endure God's timing. This is where Jesus's role as truth-teller is key. Either he tells the truth or he doesn't.

In *The Chronicles of Narnia,* C. S. Lewis presents this faith challenge in a beautiful story about Aslan the lion and a self-centered boy named Eustace. When rations were low on their ship, Eustace neglected to share what little food was available, which led to contention between him and his shipmates. He even tried to sneak an extra portion without them knowing. When they finally reached shore, Eustace slipped away instead of doing his share of the physical labor. He was concerned only with himself.

Wandering about, he discovered a dragon's cave full of gold and riches. He climbed atop the pile of treasure and imagined comfort and wealth. For some time, he pondered ways to take as much as possible for himself and daydreamed about his new find. Eventually he fell comfortably asleep.

When he awoke, he made a horrible discovery: "Sleeping on a dragon's hoard with greedy, dragonish thoughts in his heart, he had become a dragon himself."[15]

Soon after this, Eustace met a lion named Aslan who led him to a large bath full of clear water. Because of a wound that Eustace had sustained on account of his greed, he desired to step into the pool to ease the pain. Aslan told him that he must undress first.

Eustace found that he could scratch off not only the outer scales, but his whole outer dragon skin. It felt wonderful! Once he had finished, he looked at his old covering and realized how nasty it was. As he moved again to the water, he found that another layer of scales and skin was right where the first was a minute ago. This too he removed. And then a third time he stripped another layer. Frustrated and believing that he would never finish such a daunting task, he heard Aslan request to do the undressing.

Aslan was a mysterious lion, and Eustace was afraid of the harm it could do, but he finally submitted:

"The very first tear he made was so deep that I thought it had gone right into my heart. And when he began pulling the skin off, it hurt worse than anything I've ever felt. The only thing that made me able to bear it was just the pleasure of feeling the stuff peel off. You know—if you've ever picked the scab of a sore place. It hurts like billy-oh but it is such fun to see it coming away. . . . Then he caught hold of me—I didn't like that much for I was very tender underneath now that I'd no skin on—and threw me into the water. . . . I'd turned into a boy again."[16]

This, Eustace exclaimed, was "perfectly delicious."

When we have the privilege of seeing our own scales, we may work to remove them, but the difficulty can easily dissuade us from continuing. Furthermore, surrendering the protection they provide requires vulnerability. While trust is paramount here, it can be frightening to submit to God's provision and care. We're not always sure that he will take care of us. (I wonder if this is because we know how rarely and insufficiently we care for others in the ways they most need it.)

Ironically, it is a sort of faith that allows us to believe in the SimGospel. Of course, SimGospel faith is easy to attain, because it is tangible and immediate and has few associations with risk. Moreover, there are plenty of daily reminders that a SimGod is present with us, listening and promising to meet our needs.

But trusting that God is who he says he is may be the most difficult challenge of all. Even Adam and Eve lost sight of this. We will not be able to move beyond our insecurities, live well in community, or encourage kingdom building (i.e., live as Sim-Gospel heretics) until we believe that God's good word about who we are is greater than the false word that simulates it.

10

Reacclimating

It is not an easy life. The journey is long and hard, and fraught with very real dangers which must be overcome.

Richard Peace[1]

From home to Oz and back again

In the movie *The Wizard of Oz,* Dorothy had an identity crisis and left Kansas. She didn't know who or whose she was, and the promise of fulfillment caught her attention. She wanted a safe place, and she wanted remedies for her painful life at home. Oz seemed perfect. There, she didn't have to feel like a rejected orphan. Instead, she could be the center of attention. She could leave miserable Kansas behind and lose herself in this happy, new land.

What she didn't expect, however, was homesickness. Increasingly, Dorothy realized that Oz was not reality and that real joy could not be found there. She began to want the flat

Midwest and her crabby neighbor, Miss Gulch. She longed to return to Aunt Em and Uncle Henry.

But how is it that the place she most wanted to leave became the place to which she most wanted to return? What facilitated this change in perspective? Furthermore, did it require a new mind-set for her to live in Kansas again, this time as if it were like no place on earth?

Seeing behind the Wizard's curtain revealed that the savior she had been looking for was only a simulation. She had believed that Oz would magically solve her problems, and it did, though not as she expected. Her experience there clarified the truth. It gave Dorothy reference points for reality, and in the end she discovered the truth of Oz, Kansas, and herself.

When I use a compass to navigate through the woods, it is extremely important to monitor my course regularly. With only one degree of error, I will miss a target by ninety-three feet after just one mile of hiking. Consider how lost I would be after five or ten miles. Yet one degree of error seems so minuscule! Without reference points between A and B, I cannot know if I'm still heading in the right direction.

Dorothy's longing for home didn't occur until she discovered what being away from it was like. And she didn't discover what being away was like until her dream-time in Oz gave her a comparison from which to know the reality of Kansas. Navigating through a culture that is decorated, influenced, perpetuated, and preached at by a second-rate message system is much the same. We need a reality compass to make our way through the simulation presented in so much media and advertising.

As individuals and community members, we have been called to a reality that thrives on worship and care. Unfortunately, we often embrace a variation that thrives on ignorance, self-worship, and consumption. We rarely notice this misdirection because we are too distracted by the surplus and glamour of Oz—of the SimGospel. We have lost touch with who we are as God's beloved children. In the meantime, all of life is affected: how we shop, pray, measure security, perceive ourselves in the mirror, react to peer pressure, regard the poor, dignify women, value material goods, treat enemies, and view the Sabbath. Reacclimating to home takes faith that God is gracious enough to lead us there. But it is not enough to simply understand *what* or *where* home is, or *how much* we need it. Activity is necessary. In chapter 9, I mentioned some media resources and a handful of individual and group ideas that would be helpful. Below are several broader ideas that counteract the SimGospel's influence. Some of them may be quite difficult, but with time and a growing vision for God's kingdom, they are certainly doable:

• Go with a mission team to a developing or Third World country.
• Volunteer at a local mission or soup kitchen through the winter months.
• Cap your income at a rate that provides adequate provision and nothing more.
• Donate to an organization that buys cows for milk and wells for water for impoverished villages.[2] Couples are doing this at an increasing rate instead of giving table favors at wedding receptions.
• Set your lifestyle at 75 percent of the wage you earn, and use the surplus to provide for a family who makes only 50 percent of your total income. Contact a program like Habitat for Humanity for supplying mortgage assistance to low-income, first-time homeowners.[3]
• Give away your old car instead of trying to make $500 from it.
• Consider and respond to Richard Foster's challenging comments on tithing:

> The [Old Testament] tithe simply is not a sufficiently radical concept to embody the carefree unconcern for possessions that marks life in the Kingdom of God. Jesus Christ

is the Lord of all our goods, not just ten percent. It is quite possible to obey the law of the tithe without ever dealing with our mammon lust.[4]

- Buy locally grown vegetables, and fruit that is in season.
- Turn off your television long enough to hear the voice of reality speaking, and learn new ways to entertain guests. Don't let the TV take the following role in your living room:

> The TV, it seems, is the great social mediator in our household, as I suppose it is in many of the world's households. To be without it is to be without our one shared community, without our shared friends—the beautiful people of TV world. When it comes on, the room shrinks to the size of the glass screen and a limitless, dynamic other-world opens up. We plop ourselves down, plug in, exert our remaining power over the remote control, and interface with the one great human space that we still do share.[5]

I doubt that Jesus wants advertising or television to disappear. They are not simply evil, and they don't make the world an evil place. They just need a reality check. As Christians, we have a responsibility to engage with popular culture and to provide reference points—a witness—for others to see the Gospel (and to remind ourselves how easily we stray).

But we need to get through the kind of identity crisis Dorothy had. We need to accept that we are made in God's image and that we are loved by him unconditionally. As we take on his likeness, we will find increasing strength to care for our neighbors. The workplace will experience transformation that reflects the kingdom. And the church will become an active and prophetic voice in the world, without actually conforming to the world.

By trusting in Christ's wisdom to lead, and in his care to recover us when we settle for the sovereignty of a block of wood, we will see his prayer come to life:

"On earth, as it is in heaven . . ."

Notes

Introduction

1. David Cassidy, "The Areopagus Model: Let's Get Spiritual," *New Christendom Journal* 3 (2). http://www.newchristendom.com/issue11/cassidy.php.

2. Mars Hill Audio homepage, www.marshillaudio.org.

3. Neil Postman, *Amusing Ourselves to Death: Public Discourse in the Age of Show Business* (New York: Penguin, 1985), 79.

4. Stuart Ewen, *All Consuming Images: The Politics of Style in Contemporary Culture*, rev. ed. (New York: Basic Books, 1999), 103.

Chapter 1: Stolen Goods

1. *Merriam-Webster's Collegiate Dictionary*, 10th ed., s.v. "gospel."

2. Cornelius Plantinga, *Not the Way It's Supposed to Be: A Breviary of Sin* (Grand Rapids: Eerdmans, 1995), 89.

3. Jean Kilbourne, *Can't Buy My Love: How Advertising Changes the Way We Think and Feel* (New York: Touchstone, 1999), 262.

4. Stuart Ewen, as quoted in *The Ad and the Ego,* 57 min., producer/director Harold Boihem, Parallax Pictures, 1996.

Chapter 2: An Image Bearer

1. Brennan Manning, *Abba's Child: The Cry of the Heart for Intimate Belonging* (Colorado Springs: NavPress, 1994), 57.

2. David F. D'Alessandro, *Brand Warfare: 10 Rules for Building the Killer Brand* (New York: McGraw-Hill, 2001), 23.

3. Ibid.

4. Henri J. M. Nouwen, *Reaching Out: The Three Movements of the Spiritual Life* (New York: Doubleday, 1975, 1986), 111.

5. Manning, *Abba's Child*, 50–51.

6. Bernard McGrane, as quoted in *The Ad and the Ego*.

Chapter 3: A Needs Bearer

1. Abraham Maslow, *Motivation and Personality* (New York: Harper & Row, 1954).

2. Sut Jhally, as quoted in *The Ad and the Ego*.

3. Tim Kasser, *High Price of Materialism* (Cambridge: MIT Press, 2002), 24.

4. Anne Bradstreet, from "The Vanity of All Worldly Things," *Discovering Literature: Fiction, Poetry, and Drama,* Hans P. Guth and Gabriele L. Rico, eds. (Englewood Cliffs, NJ: Blair Press, 1993), 444.

5. Fr. Reginald Garrigou-Lagrange, *Life Everlasting and the Immensity of the Soul* (Rockford, IL: Tan Books, 1952), 10.

6. Plantinga, *Not the Way*, 33.

Chapter 4: A Finicky Follower

1. www.look-look.com. For more information on cool hunting, go to www.pbs.org and watch the excellent PBS Frontline special "Merchants of Cool," produced by Barak Goodman and Rachel Dretzin (February 27, 2001). A teacher's guide is available.

2. See Malcolm Gladwell, "The Coolhunt," *New Yorker* (March 17, 1997), section 2, for more on the terms "Innovators," "Early Adopters," "Majority," and the diffusion research cycle regarding cool hunting.

3. Bill McKibben, *Age of Missing Information* (New York: Plume, 1992), 228.

4. Maria Shriver, "Jamie Lee Curtis Keeps It Real," NBC, *Dateline* (September 15, 2002). See www.thats-a-wrap.net/jlc/jlcdateline.shtml for complete interview.

5. Jean Kilbourne, as quoted in *The Ad and the Ego*.

6. Ibid.

7. Bernard McGrane, as quoted in *The Ad and the Ego*.

8. *Tommy Boy*, 97 min., produced by Robert K. Weiss, directed by Peter Segal, Paramount Pictures, 1995.

9. *It's a Wonderful Life*, 130 min., produced/directed by Frank Capra, Liberty Films, 1946.

10. C. S. Lewis, *The Weight of Glory* (San Francisco: HarperSanFrancisco, 2001), 26.

11. William H. Willimon and Thomas H. Naylor, *The Abandoned Generation: Rethinking Higher Education* (Grand Rapids: Eerdmans, 1995), 38–39.

12. M. P. Dunleavey, "The Hidden Costs of Too Much Stuff," MSN Money, http://moneycentral.msn.com/content/SavingandDebt/P43217.asp.

Chapter 5: An Image Bearer Next Door

1. John Piper, *Desiring God: Meditations of a Christian Hedonist,* rev. ed. (Sisters, OR: Multnomah, 1986, 1996).

2. Richard M. Gula, S.S., *The Good Life: Where Morality and Spirituality Converge* (New York: Paulist Press, 1999), 16.

3. Richard M. Gula, S.S., *Reason Informed by Faith: Foundations of Catholic Ministry* (New York: Paulist Press, 1989), 65.

4. Christine D. Pohl, *Making Room: Recovering Hospitality as a Christian Tradition* (Grand Rapids: Eerdmans, 1999), 21.

5. See chapter 4 above.

6. Center for Substance Abuse Prevention, Prevention Pathways: Online Courses, "It Won't Happen to Me," http://pathwayscourses.samhsa.gov/vawc/vawc_5_pg7.htm.

7. Kilbourne, as quoted in *The Ad and the Ego.*

8. Lilian Calles Barger, *Eve's Revenge: Women and a Spirituality of the Body* (Grand Rapids: Brazos Press, 2003), 44.

9. Ibid., 46.

10. Ibid., 47.

11. Dr. Ann Hagmann, *Climbing the Sycamore Tree: A Study on Choice and Simplicity* (Nashville: Upper Room Books, 2001), 52.

12. Ibid.

Chapter 6: A Needs Bearer Next Door

1. Steven Garber, "Making Sense of a Movie," *Critique: Helping Christians Develop Skill in Discernment,* no. 4, 8.

2. Eugene H. Peterson, *The Message: The New Testament in Contemporary Language* (Colorado Springs: NavPress, 1993).

3. Garber, "Making Sense," 9.

4. *Merriam-Webster's,* s.v. "amuse."

5. Pohl, *Making Room,* 13.

6. Ibid., 5.

7. Nouwen, *Reaching Out,* 122.

8. The Enron whistle-blower, Sherron Watkins, was reportedly a Christian.

9. Willimon, *The Abandoned Generation,* 38.

10. *Merriam-Webster's,* s.v. "calling."

11. Brian Walsh, "How to Think Your Way through College," *HIS,* November 1983, 28.

12. Frederick Buechner, *Wishful Thinking: A Theological ABC* (San Francisco: Harper-SanFrancisco, 1973), 95.

13. Piper, *Desiring God,* 9.

14. Ibid., 46.

Chapter 7: A Neglected Member

1. Peterson, *The Message.*

2. Steven Garber, *The Fabric of Faithfulness: Weaving Together Belief & Behavior during the University Years* (Downers Grove, IL: InterVarsity Press, 1996).

3. Thomas Aquinas, O.P., *Summa theologica,* II–II, q. 66, a. 2.

4. See www.redefiningprogress.org.

Notes

5. Susan Reifer, "Watch Your Step: How to Leave the Smallest 'Footprint' Possible," *Vegetarian Times,* April 2002, 42.

6. *Shanghai Star,* "Bigger Portions Equal Bigger Americans," January 30, 2003, http://app1.chinadaily.com.cn/star/2003/0130/he19-4.html.

7. Reifer, "Watch Your Step," 43.

8. J. R. R. Tolkien, *The Hobbit; or, There and Back Again,* rev. ed. (New York: Ballantine Books, 1966, 1996).

9. Naomi Klein, *No Logo* (New York: Picador, 2000, 2002), 202.

10. www.exchangerate.com.

11. Klein, *No Logo,* 202.

12. Ron Sider, *Rich Christians in an Age of Hunger: Moving from Affluence to Generosity,* rev. ed. (Nashville: W. Publishing Group, 1997), 174.

13. Jean C. Lough, "Gateways to the Promised Land: The Role Played by the Southern Kansas Towns in the Opening of the Cherokee Strip to Settlement," *Kansas Historical Quarterly* 25 (Spring 1959), 17–31.

14. Lough, quote taken from the *Denver Republican,* September 18, 1893.

15. Kilbourne, as quoted in *The Ad and the Ego.*

Chapter 8: Becoming like Christ

1. Hagmann, *Climbing the Sycamore Tree,* 44.

2. I want to be clear that becoming like Christ is not something we do entirely on our own. This chapter only highlights elements that we can practice in response to our Christian calling.

3. *The Truman Show,* 103 min., produced by Edward S. Feldman, et al., directed by Peter Weir, Paramount Pictures, 1998.

4. Manning, *Abba's Child.*

5. Henri Nouwen, "Bringing Solitude into Our Lives," *Devotional Classics: Selected Readings for Individuals and Groups,* ed. Richard J. Foster and James Bryan Smith (San Francisco: HarperSanFrancisco, 1990, 1991, 1993), 96.

6. Nouwen, *Reaching Out,* 141.

7. Ignatian spirituality serves the broader purpose of assisting retreatants in discerning calling. A full-scale retreat would take four weeks, each week focusing on a different stage of Jesus's life. I have included only a few elements that can be used at any time for reading scripture.

8. Spelled out in the Apostles' and Nicene creeds.

9. Nouwen, *Reaching Out,* 136.

10. Peterson, *The Message.*

11. Nouwen, *Reaching Out,* 137.

12. Gula, *The Good Life,* 14.

13. Gula, *Reason Informed by Faith,* 64.

Chapter 9: Becoming a SimGospel Heretic

1. As quoted in *The Ad and the Ego.*

2. Some critics (Roger Ebert of the *Chicago Sun-Times,* James Berardinelli of *ReelViews,* etc.) believe that this film is a modern parallel to the Christ story. Its symbolism certainly

supports this claim. *The Green Mile* is the second Stephen King story to be directed by Frank Darabont. The first was *The Shawshank Redemption*.

3. Based on the book by Sister Helen Prejean, this award-winning film has, as its climax, a convicted rapist committing his life to Christ. Director Tim Robbins saw the defining characteristics of this movie as redemption and Jesus's call to "love your enemies." For more insights, see *Dead Man Walking: The Shooting Script* (New York: Newmarket Press, 1997).

4. Kilbourne, *Can't Buy My Love*, 107.

5. William D. Romanowski, *Eyes Wide Open: Looking for God in Popular Culture* (Grand Rapids: Brazos Press, 2001).

6. See www.breakpoint.org.

7. See www.ransomfellowship.org. *Critique* is available by donation to Ransom Fellowship, 1150 West Center, Rochester, MN 55902.

8. The 2004 TV-Turnoff week boasted 7.63 million participants. See www.tvturnoff. org for more information on this nonprofit organization.

9. See www.commercialalert.org for more information. When you sign on, this organization will provide regular notices on justice issues related to media. Links and formatted letters (to governing officials, etc.) will allow you to easily support or protest specific issues.

10. Darren Rovell, "Baseball Scales Back Movie Promotion," ESPN.com, http://sports.espn.go.com/espn/sportsbusiness/news/story?id=1796765 (May 6, 2004).

11. Kilbourne, as quoted in *The Ad and the Ego*.

12. Integrating an ad study with biblical principles is my method of choice, and there are many engaging ways to do it: for example, week one, study specific scripture passages; week two, critique ads related to that scripture; week three, discuss relationship between weeks one and two. Sometimes, however, your group may not be open to "church talk." In this case, it is helpful just to get participants thinking. In the future, they may be open to a scripture approach.

13. *The Ad and the Ego* can be found at www.parallax.com, or through interlibrary loan. For a list of excellent documentaries related to advertising and its effects, visit the Media Education Foundation at www.mediaed.org.

14. *Indiana Jones and the Last Crusade*, 127 min., produced by George Lucas et al., directed by Steven Spielberg, Lucasfilm Ltd. and Paramount Pictures, 1989.

15. C. S. Lewis, *The Chronicles of Narnia*, bk. 5: *The Voyage of the Dawn Treader* (New York: HarperTrophy, 1952, 1980), 97.

16. Ibid., 116.

Chapter 10: Reacclimating

1. Richard V. Peace, *Pilgrimage: A Handbook on Christian Growth* (Grand Rapids: Baker, 1976, 1984), 18.

2. See www.heifer.org to learn about this ministry.

3. See www.habitat.org for more information on this Christian nonprofit organization.

4. Richard J. Foster, *Freedom of Simplicity* (New York: HarperPaperbacks, 1981), 62–63.

5. Richard DeGrandpre, "United We Sit," *Adbusters*, no. 45, January/February 2003.